Earthbound Angel

Earthbound Angel

Christy Shackleford

RESOURCE *Publications* · Eugene, Oregon

EARTHBOUND ANGEL

Resource Publications
An Imprint of Wipf and Stock Publishers
199 W. 8th Ave., Suite 3
Eugene, OR 97401

www.wipfandstock.com

PAPERBACK ISBN: 978-1-6667-0535-5
HARDCOVER ISBN: 978-1-6667-0536-2
EBOOK ISBN: 978-1-6667-0537-9

Dedication

Before I start on the endeavor of writing what is the most important collection of words that have ever come from my fingertips, I want to mention a few of the people who have made this task both conceivable and possible for me.

First and foremost, it is with all my humble praise and honor that I dedicate *Earthbound Angel* to my Lord and Savior Jesus Christ and his Holy Spirit. Because of their unfailing love for me, I have been given the gift of salvation and eternal life.

Next and with all my love I dedicate this story to my husband, Jon. Because of him, I have grown into the woman that I am. It is because of his persistence and his love that I have the confidence to do what the Lord has asked me to do. He is my soulmate and my love!

The third dedication I have is to my son Danny (Jeremiah Daniel). Since I was nineteen, he has been the constant in my life. From infancy to adulthood, he has been my joy, my friend, my son. Danny, you must realize that even though this book is for your sister, it takes nothing away from my love and pride that I have for you.

Finally, to my daughter Jonna. Her life has brought me great happiness, true friendship, daily heartfelt conversations, and a multitude of tears and laughter. She has shown me that the meaning of "I can do all things through Christ who strengthens me" (Phil 4:13) really means what it says. But most of all, she has given me the knowledge and thankfulness that the love of a mother and daughter surely does extend the barriers of time and distance. This love knows no limits and can never be exhausted or lost.

Table of Contents

Preface

Scripture tells me that all words in the Bible are inspired by the Holy Spirit; therefore, they are reliable, true, and can be believed. The words I write are neither divine nor Scriptural. They are words describing an event in my life that I have been commissioned by the Lord Jesus to share with whomever will have listening ears. However, these words are relayed to me by the Holy Spirit of my Lord Jesus since I can do nothing without him.

For thirteen years, the Holy Spirit told me that I would write this book. Even though I received this knowledge thirteen years ago, I understood that the timing would be directed by my Lord . . . not myself. As of this moment, I realize that this is the time. Now is the season of my life that I will draw from the deepest holes in my heart. Scripture says, "I can do all things through Christ who strengthens me," Philippians 4:13.

As I sit at this keyboard, I am relying on the grace and mercy of my Lord Jesus to take over my fingers and dictate the words he wishes me to share. I am only the messenger . . . a messenger who has walked through the life event that, for whatever reason, the Lord chose me for. However, after trotting down the narrowest and darkest path I could ever imagine, and one that I said I could never handle, I am sitting here because I have kept my eyes on Jesus and I have trusted him with all that I am. He is my light in a world of darkness. To him I give all glory, honor, praise, and love.

Praise God in His sanctuary;
Praise Him in His mighty firmament!
Praise Him for His mighty acts;
Praise Him according to His excellent greatness!
Praise Him with the sound of the trumpet;

ix

Praise Him with the lute and the harp!
Praise Him with the timbrel and dance;
Praise Him with stringed instruments and flutes
Praise Him with loud cymbals; Praise Him with clashing cymbals!
Let everything that has breath praise the Lord.
Praise the Lord!

Praise Him with loud cymbals; Praise Him with clashing cymbals!
Let everything that has breath praise the Lord.
Praise the Lord!

—Psalm 150

Chapter One

The Desire of My Heart

WHERE DO I BEGIN to tell a story that is wrapped up within my heart so tightly that I can scarcely breathe at times? Perhaps the only way is to start from the beginning.

On February 26, 1982, Jon and I were married. It was a second marriage for both of us. As a result of that, Jon not only married me, but he married my son, who was the most precious and cutest little four-year-old boy named Danny. Danny and I were no longer a twosome—we were a family. Jon did not have children from his previous marriage, so he instantly became a dad to Danny. We were happy as a family, but something was missing. I knew that we needed another baby, but I decided I would wait for Jon to broach that subject.

We lived in a town in southern Illinois, where I had grown up and Jon had lived since he was nine years old, as his family originated in the hills of Missouri. Soon after his high school graduation, he went to work out of the Ironworker's Local in Evansville, Indiana. Because of the distance involved between Harrisburg, Illinois, and the places he was sent to work (mostly in Indiana and Kentucky), my son Danny and I did not see a lot of him until the weekends.

I will never forget the night that my story truly begins. It was a Friday night in the spring of April 1982. Jon had worked that day, and then drove an hour and a half to Evansville for a union meeting. It was late when his little white Pinto pulled into the driveway of our small but cozy house. Danny was sound asleep in his bed, but I was waiting up for Jon. Not long after my husband of two months walked into the door, dirty and tired from his long, work-filled day, he told me he had something on his mind. To my delight, Jon thought we should start trying to have a baby of

1

our own. "Wow," I thought, "the Lord didn't take very long to answer my prayer for Jon to want a baby."

I use the word "trying" because I had already informed him that during my previous marriage it had taken me almost a year and a half of "trying" and praying before I was able to conceive. We decided that we should start "trying" that night, though neither one of us expected the result that occurred. After Jon had gone to sleep, I went outside and sat on the front porch step to enjoy the cool, spring night. It was a clear night. I looked up at the stars and remember thinking how awesome it was that my Jesus knew them all by name. The crickets were singing around me in rhythm and harmony, and every once in a while I heard a cat or dog singing along with them. There was a definite chill that spring night, but I was surprisingly warm. I sat on that step and thought about how very much I loved my husband, and after a while, I decided I would talk to Jesus about the decision Jon and I had made.

In short, Jesus listened to my prayer.

Within what seemed like a few minutes, the Holy Spirit quieted me and deep within my soul, I heard my Lord speak the very words to me, "My child, there will be a baby. She will be special." None could imagine the joy that I felt in that very moment. Not only did the still, small voice of my Lord tell me I would have another child, he said "She!" In my bliss, I started thanking my Lord Jesus. All of a sudden, I stopped thanking and praising him for his answer to me, and I noticed that alongside the physical warmth I felt on that spring night, I also felt a warmth inside comparable to the feeling I would get as a little girl when my daddy would wrap his strong arms around me. I felt safe, secure, and loved by my Lord Jesus, because it seemed at that moment, his arms had engulfed my entire body, soul, and mind. I could hear his words far more clearly than I hear my own. He told me this baby would be special, and boy, do I grasp now exactly what he was telling me.

Not only was I going to have a child, I was *already* pregnant with her—something so precious in that very moment was already growing inside of me. Not only was my own flesh and blood now growing within me, this was the same little girl that my Jesus had referred to as "special!" during my talks with God.

Even though I was ecstatic over the miracle of that night, I decided to keep it to myself for a little while. I decided that I would wait until I had confirmation from my doctor to tell a soul. While it was a difficult task to do, I was strong-willed and determined enough to not let it slip from my mouth. For a couple of weeks, I would watch the days on the calendar creep up to my "time of month." Finally, that time arrived, and nothing happened. For most of you reading this story, that won't come as a surprise to you, because you already know that I have faith at least "the size of a mustard seed." I was absolutely overjoyed and decided I would go to the pharmacy and purchase a pregnancy test. As soon as I got home, I rushed to find out what the results would be. I took a deep breath, gave Jesus my gratitude again, and read the directions on the package, doing just as it told. The anticipation grew until I finally had my answer.

I was pregnant! I *knew* it! I had felt it! I had believed it! Tears of joy streamed down my face, and I could finally reveal the news to my husband Jon.

After I spread the news all around to everyone—my husband, Danny, family, and friends, I immediately called the doctor to make an appointment. The next day, I went to the lab, gave them my blood, and the doctor informed me that I was not pregnant. He said to come back in about a week, and I could try the test again. I left, disappointed but not dejected. I remembered a Scripture in the Bible where the Apostle Paul said, "We are hard-pressed on every side, yet not crushed; we are perplexed, but not in despair; persecuted, but not forsaken; struck down, but not destroyed" (2 Corinthians 4:8–9). Yes, I was heartbroken that the test results were not as I expected. But I was not going to give up on the Lord's promise that I was pregnant. The Lord's word is his word, and his Word is his promise. I believed this with all my heart.

The next week, I diligently reported back to the doctor's office and once again gave my blood to the lab technician. Once again, the doctor reported that I was *not* pregnant. I was not prepared for this prognosis, and I very politely yet sternly told the doctor that he didn't know what he was talking about because I definitely was pregnant. He was very compassionate, and kindly informed me that I needed to come back in a few more days. In my mind, I understood his words, "a few more days" to mean exactly that, so the very next morning, I called the lab and set up an appointment. After waiting patiently for a mere twenty-four hours more, I trotted off to the lab to hand over another yet vial of my A-positive blood. Since this was round three, the sweet lady that took my blood knew what the results were, she felt. Without the delay of writing a lab report, without the protocol of sending a report to the doctor, and without granting me an hour or two of suspense, she very gently smiled and finally confirmed that I was pregnant. I began crying as my heart rejoiced, and my mouth responded with the words, "I knew it, Jesus!" The woman wearing a white lab coat grinned yet again. In agreement with me, she said, "We knew it all along!" Without waiting to see the doctor, I hurried home to call Jon.

This time my A-positive blood confirmed it. This time I could prove to everyone that it was true. This time, what I knew in my heart was going to be shown to the world.

This time, I was indeed going to give birth to a special baby girl whose name was Jonna Christine Shackleford.

Chapter Two

The Arrival

THE NEXT MONTHS WERE incredibly blessed, and why wouldn't they be? There was a miracle growing within my body. Greater still was the miracle that was within my heart and my spirit. During the next several months, my spirit connected to that of my precious baby. This baby was part of me, all that I was. The little heartbeat was strong and steady. It stayed around 154 beats per minute, faster than Danny's, which hovered around 130. As the baby grew, I felt little flutters that resembled "butterfly wings" against the inside of my stomach. I remembered from my first pregnancy that this was one of many classic signs of the baby's movement.

As the baby grew, I quickly became aware of a startling fact: that she was either growing faster than normal, or else I was gaining a bunch of extra weight. With Danny, I gained twenty-three pounds in my lower portions, and what seemed like overnight the twenty-three pounds went as quickly as it came. At first, I was not a happy mother when the doctor politely informed me that I needed to monitor what I ate.

I watched it all right!

I watched food go right into my mouth. I remember repeating to myself that I surely wouldn't gain that much. But Baby Shackleford was hungry all the time whereas I only craved one thing with Danny—popcorn. However, Danny's little sibling was craving anything and everything. I blamed it on the baby's desire to eat like it would justify my desire to eat, so by the end of nine months, this momma was perfectly plump. I can honestly say that I believe even the hair on my head got fatter. However many inches I put on my feet, legs, bottom, etc., they were no match to the inches padded onto my belly.

When the due date for Baby Shackleford came and went, Jon had to assist me in getting in and out of cars, chairs, and bathtubs. I have no idea how many inches were added onto my physique, but I do know that by January 15, 1983, I had put on a whopping sixty-five pounds.

January 15 arrived, and the baby just wasn't ready to be born into this world. Many family members and friends offered theories that would bring on the labor process, and many of those opinions offered were tested. Needless to say, they were theories never proven true. The days passed by, the pounds piled on, the heartbeat of the unique creation was sure and steady. Baby gymnastics stopped because there was no longer any room in the arena. As a result, the little Shackleford bundle resorted to kicking me in the kidneys. Between trips to the bathroom, swollen body parts, and an irregular, well, everything, this momma was more than ready to see the precious face of the little miracle that I had already come to know.

Since my due date had produced no baby, I was in the doctor's office every three days to monitor any progression. There were no talks of a possible C-section because neither the baby nor I showed signs of distress according to the doctor. If you would have asked my husband and six-year old-son, they would have told you that my attitude was in full distress mode. I know I was hard to live with. Anybody carrying seventy-three extra pounds of "baby" would be. Right? Although the days of feeling like a giant hippopotamus kept piling up, I still maintained joy and peace that shrouded around me on that cool night last April when I felt the strengthening presence of my Lord Jesus. That was the night that he and I talked while sitting on the front porch steps of our little house. That was the night that I conceived this absolute miracle within me.

At 4:12 a.m. and after only six hours of labor, the proper introduction between mother and child was official. Baby Shackleford came joyfully into this word weighing eight pounds, 1.6 ounces, and measuring twenty-one inches long. The baby that took up all available space within my belly for nine months now slept peacefully, wrapped up in a white baby blanket securely protected from the world around her by the loving embrace of her momma's arms. This was the little one that the Lord specifically meant would be "special." This was no longer Baby Shackleford. In a matter of nine and a half months, this baby finally had a name to address her wonderful heavenly little spirit.

On January 29, 1983, Jonna Christine Shackleford entered this world to forever change it. Never did I realize the importance of Jesus' words to me that night in April nor realize the truth in God's word that he directs our path. Never did I realize the literal meaning God's words to Jeremiah the Prophet:

"Before I formed you in the womb, I knew you; before you were born, I sanctified you," Jeremiah 1:12.

Never did I realize the road that lay before me.

Never could I realize how treacherous that road would be.

Never could I realize . . .

Chapter Three

Introduction to the World

WHERE DO I GO from here? Jonna's birth was so uncomplicated. She was a perfect baby, and even though I may be partial, she was absolutely beautiful! From her daddy's genetics, she inherited his dark brown, almost blackish hair and a deep complexion that mimicked the Native American Cherokee that was embedded into her ancestry.

Jonna's daddy tells the story that while he was admiring his daughter outside of the nursery window after her birth, there was another family waiting to see the newest addition to their family. They were a lovely biracial family, as the father was African American and the mother was Caucasian. The family was quite excited when they discovered the newly born little girl bearing their name. However, the name tags were not easily seen through the thickened glass that separated families from their babies. But coincidence would have it that this family happened to live down the street from us! I knew their child was due, but what were the chances of my little girl and theirs being birthed on the same day?

Jon and our neighbor started discussing the birth of the two babies. Within seconds, Jon realized something was quite amiss, for our neighbors had thought our little Jonna was actually their child. They had surmised that little girl in the nursery was surely theirs; however, this was not the case. The baby behind that clear glass was our own little bundle. Jonna's Native American ancestry was glowing far more intensely than the African American roots of the only other little girl born that day. Well, all involved shared quite a good laugh about the mistake as did I, too, as soon as Jon told me. By the way, both little girls shared in the gifts of beauty.

Immediately after Jonna's introduction into the world outside of her safe, secure home within her mother, I could see the intense glare popping from her eyes. It was as if she was already taking in and analyzing her surroundings—as if she was already on a mission to understand the world she was now destined to be part of.

My bloodline did not offer much. The Irish, German, and English mix didn't seem to have taken hold in this newborn baby of mine. I always held to the fact that she had her momma's chin, but I do believe that it was only a figment of my imagination. After a closer examination, however, I found that my baby inherited a distinct trait of me that nobody else could possibly claim: she had undeniably inherited my toes! Even more remarkable than that, I have always had a little birthmark the size of a freckle on the tip of my left big toe. My perfect newborn daughter received the same birthmark on the tip of her right big toe. Hallelujah! I felt very relieved to know that my little bundle of joy did, in fact, belong to me.

After an overnight stay in the hospital, Jon and Danny came to take me and the new addition to the Shackleford family home. Nothing out of the ordinary happened at 312 E. McIlrath Street, except now we were a family of four.

Daily routines were established quickly. Jonna nursed, diapers were changed, baths were given, Jonna nursed, diapers changed, and more baths were given. And again and again. As in other households, a newborn doesn't always take precedence because of husbands and siblings. But Danny was almost six years old and in first grade. As a result, most of the day was spent doing household chores in the company of just Jonna and me. Danny was so very helpful after school was out and would play with his sister, change diapers for momma, and often help with dinner (he is forty-three now and still loves to cook). Daddy's domestic tasks, on the other hand, were a little more complicated. As an ironworker (high steel construction worker) employed out of Evansville, Indiana, local, he was either asleep, driving at a pretty good clip down the highway in order to be at work on time, or at work. The routine this devoted daddy executed every day didn't allow much time to help Mom with the tasks of motherhood. His work schedule demanded that he get up around 4:00 a.m. in order to drive to work, and Jonna did not like that schedule. In fact, she didn't like anyone's schedule. Her idea of naps consisted of sleeping forty-five minutes. She was under the false impression that nighttime only required sleeping in forty-five-minute intervals as well. So, in order for Jon and Danny to be able to sleep, I would go to bed after my babies were all tucked in for the night and under the false illusion that the night time kisses and I love yous were finished.

Sure enough, after a very brief—I do mean very brief—slumber, my precious night owl would let the stars in the heavens know she was awake. Night after night, this schedule dominated. I soon learned that the only way to keep peace in the family was to stay up with her and rock. We would rock, or should I say I would rock as Jonna would sleep in my arms. You see, the forty-five minutes would spread into hours as long as I rocked. Believe me, that old red recliner rocker and I developed a comfortable relationship. For about a year, Jonna slept in my arms at night while I rocked her and watched Nickelodeon on TV. I truthfully enjoyed watching the black-and white-reruns of *I Love Lucy*, *Bewitched*, *Father Knows Best*, *Leave It to Beaver*, and *Andy Griffith*, as they were the shows I watched as a little girl. Yes, I realize I am revealing my age, but that's okay! Anyway, time went on, and Jonna learned to sleep in her baby bed with various stuffed animals. Danny appreciated her slumber, as they shared a room.

All of her life, Jonna was like a sponge and eager to learn about anything and everything! She was certainly the most determined infant I had
ever seen, and I remember when she was four months old, we completely
moved out of our house into my grandmother's basement apartment. Jon
and a friend stripped the house down to the frame to remodel it, and
while I was at the house trying to help some, Jonna stayed with her great-
grandma, Mammy. When I returned to the apartment, my Mammy had
taught Jonna to sit up. Though that is nothing out of the ordinary, two
weeks later, after moving back into our little house with new walls and
carpet, Danny started walking his little sister around the house holding
her hands. Soon after, she was walking solo. Yep, Danny's six-month-
old baby sister was now walking alone. I didn't think too much about
that either at the time. I realized it was early, but Danny walked at seven
months. Maybe it can be attributed to all the love and encouragement
that I made sure they received.

Jonna's walking ability quickly turned into acrobatic feats that I, as
her momma, cringed to watch. One morning I was attempting to pick up
the house and noticed it was quiet—always a bad sign. I walked around
the house and couldn't find her, so my common sense told me that she
couldn't possibly have gotten outside, but I had to go check the yard regardless. Nothing!!! My little daredevil was nowhere to be found. Needless to say, my heartbeat increased to an alarming rate, and my breathing

grew rapid. All I knew to do was make an emergency call to the Indiana-based construction site where her daddy was working and then call 911. Then, my common sense, or what little I was bestowed with, kicked in and I decided to call 911 first. Panicked anyway, all I could think about was finding my Jonna.

As I walked back into the house, I heard a noise in the bedroom. After Jon remodeled the house, he and his dad built a chest of drawers into the wall of the kids' bedroom. The chest was four drawers high starting from the floor. On top of the drawers were cabinet doors hiding shelves that continued up to the ceiling. I was not surprised to discover my little girl, but I was surprised to discover the task she had committed herself to do. She had opened the bottom drawer and climbed in and then followed that pattern with the other drawers, as if making stair steps to the cabinet doors. My little angel was sitting in the top drawer, had the doors to the shelves opened where all the stuffed animals, game boxes, and various kinds of toys belonging to her and her brother were kept. There she sat, proceeding to throw anything within reach to the floor.

Then, I recall another incident when Jonna was about three years old and we had bought a swing set for the kids. Across the top of the frame were monkey bars that Danny could walk across with his hands. It looked like a ladder that was lying down on top of the frame. Jonna could "hand walk" across the bars if her daddy, brother, or I would hold her up. One particular day, the kids were outside playing in the backyard and I was occupied within the house. Having heard the phone ring, I answered it only to hear our neighbor screaming that I better get outside because Jonna was going to fall. I looked out the back door window to see what our neighbor was talking about—my heart stopped when I went out the back door. This little daredevil was walking across the monkey bars with nobody holding her up or assisting her. She had maneuvered herself up on the beam of the swing-set frame, climbed to the top of the monkey bar, and was walking with her feet across the top of the swing set.

Needless to say, Jonna could not be trusted to be alone, because there was absolutely no fear in her. As Scripture says, "Be strong and of a good courage; be not discouraged nor dismayed for the Lord thy God is with thee wheresoever thou goest," Joshua 1:9. At the time of conception, the Lord had definitely instilled a sense of physical strength and fearlessness into this child. The qualities of a future leader? I often wondered just where the Lord Jesus would lead her. I often tried to figure out just where the path our all-knowing God paved only for my Jonna would end. I often wondered . . .

Chapter Four

Competitive Spirit

THE NEXT FEW YEARS came and went without any extraordinary or unusual occurrences in Jonna's life. At four years old, we enrolled her into a preschool so that her social skills would be ready for kindergarten. Until that point in time, Jonna was pretty much a little tomboy. Sure, she loved her baby dolls, Care Bears, Barbies, My Little Ponies, coloring books, reading books, play dough, and any of her big brother's toys that she could find. But for the most part, she was surrounded by boys, and boys of all ages, as well as the next-door neighbor boys, Danny's friends, and Danny.

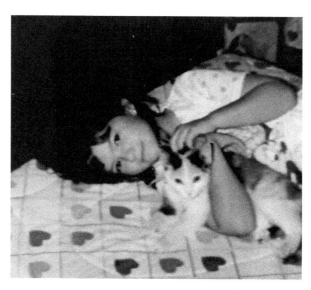

I will never forget one particular night when Danny had friends stay all night. By the end of the night, either the boys were chasing Jonna, or she was chasing the boys through our little four-room house with all of her Care Bears. For those of you readers who don't know what a Care Bear is, they were different-colored (mostly pastel colors) stuffed bears. Each bear had a different emotion and name. Believe me, we had every one of them, too. That night, Care Bears were flying, running, and doing flip flops through the usually tidy house. In Jonna's hands, it wasn't very long until the Care Bears ceased to yell, run, or fly. They had definitely been grounded. The boys and Jonna ended up tangled up in the shower curtain, along with their Care Bear. "That's enough!" I told the rowdy bunch. Have you ever tried to do homework for a Music Theory class while hearing the earth-shattering screams of Care Bears and kids? There is no benefit to the accompaniment of such musical tones while you are trying to write a Baroque-Period music composition for your final semester grade. I believe I remember that the kids calmed down and put the bears back into their cabinet for the night. In the midst of the calamity, I had to laugh, though. Such precious memories!

The year Jonna started kindergarten, Danny was in sixth grade, and that was the only year that they attended the same school together. I remember the day that school started as I sat and watched my little boy (now her big brother) and little girl walk down the sidewalk into the double doors of the elementary school. When I could no longer see them, I turned into the Hardee's parking lot, hoped nobody would see me, and sat isolated in the car while huge warm tears flowed like a waterfall down my face. Where had the time gone? Where were my babies? I cried for a while, dried my tears, blew my nose, drove through Hardee's drive-thru, and ordered breakfast.

In what seemed to be only a matter of weeks, that school year was over. Then, weeks turned into more weeks, then months, and all of a sudden years had passed. Jonna had survived five years of elementary school with only two mishaps that I remember. Both ordeals gave claim to her sixth-grade year.

The determination that she was born with gave way to a competitive spirit. She didn't mind losing, but she absolutely tried her best to never lose. One wintery morning of her last year of elementary school, she was racing a friend in the gym, and he was just a bit faster than she. As the finish line drew closer and her competitive drive increased, she went full speed ahead. Do I have to tell you that she won the race? She did! Victory was hers . . . along with a trip to two different doctors, x-rays, and a pretty purple cast as a trophy of hers.

She was so determined to win that race that she didn't calculate how close she was to the wall in front of her, and held her arm up to keep from hitting it, and the force broke her lower arm.

Yep, that was my girl.

Another notable memory I hold dear to my heart that year was when Jonna Christine Shackleford became a Christian. At eleven years old, my little girl gave her life, heart, and love to the Lord Jesus and was baptized soon after. It was a custom of the pastor of our church to come to the house and counsel newly saved pre-baptismal candidates to make sure they absolutely understood the concept of salvation. It was two weeks before he scheduled a time to talk to Jonna. During those two weeks, my precious little girl and I had several discussions. She would ask me questions about Jesus, and together, we would search for answers in Scripture. After the counseling session with the pastor, Jonna completely understood that Jesus had died in her place, had taken her sins to the cross with him, had defeated Satan by rising again on the third day, and was her Lord and Savior for all Eternity. The answers she gave our pastor that day were straightforward, knowledgeable, sincere, and passionate. My baby girl, without doubt, knew her Lord Jesus, It was at that moment that I realized that she was my baby, but she was his child.

Chapter Five

Jonna's Unfailing Love

THE SCHOOL YEAR 1995–96 was an eventful time for the Shackleford family. Danny graduated from Harrisburg High School and moved into his great-grandma's downstairs apartment. I earned my Bachelor's of Music degree from Southern Illinois University and started substitute teaching at Malan Junior High. Jonna was promoted from East Side Elementary School to Malan Junior High. It was during this year that I started noticing a change in my little girl. It was either a subtle change, or perhaps no change at all. It could have been that I was just putting the pieces of Jonna's spirituality together at that point.

She was never a sickly baby or child. A few trips to the doctor with Roseolla, ear infections, and strep throat were just about the extent of anything. Nothing unusual, right? However, since she had started elementary school, Jon and I noticed that an upset tummy turned from occasional too often. We just chalked it off to heredity symptoms, because Jon's family ate Tums as if they were candy. It wasn't until her seventh-grade year that my momma instinct began to tell me it was more than genetics.

About midway through Jonna's seventh-grade year, tummyaches increased. When I picked her up from school, it was routine that she would immediately start telling me how her day had gone. I never needed to ask. Gradually, the routine started shifting. Jonna's beaming personality began to dim. I started having to ask how the school day went, and sometimes she would openly discuss it, other times she was wound so tightly that I knew just to leave it alone. You see, even though Jonna's outward appearance was almost a mirror image of her daddy, her inward spirit contained some of her momma's traits, the good and the bad. Not forgetting the people, events, or situations which were upsetting to her was one of those "Momma things."

Through experience I completely understood that this little girl had loved school since day one of kindergarten. As I said before, she loved learning, observing, making conclusions, and dissecting life itself. Throughout her school career, she was a straight-A kind of girl and expected no less from herself. In anything she did, she had to know in her heart that she gave it her all.

I was always that way too; however, her methods for learning and studying grew vastly different. I read material and had to rewrite it to remember it. Jonna read material with a photographic memory, an uncanny ability to read, remember, and understand the slightest detail. As a result, school was a breeze for her, so to say.

Even though she didn't really want to discuss her moodiness, I felt that it was time she and I talked about what was going on inside her brain. As soon as we walked into the front door, I followed her to the bedroom, sat on the bed, pulled her into my lap, and said, "Okay, what gives?"

That day, when I asked her to tell me what was bothering her, I was definitely shocked when tears flowed down her cheeks and she revealed that she hated school. Now how was I to handle this one? What had happened to completely turn this mind who was constantly challenged to learn around 180 degrees? Being the momma that I was, I absolutely had to find out what in the world was motivating my child to use the word "hate" toward something that she had always loved.

"Why?" I asked, trying to be as calm and natural as I could.

Sitting in my lap, she grabbed hold of my neck, continued crying, and hugged me tightly. After a few minutes, she began to explain the entire scenario to me. I listened, and completely understood her reasoning even before the words were completely finished pouring out of her mouth. Jonna revealed that she didn't understand the way kids treated other kids so poorly. That particular day, in one of her classes, another classmate had deliberately pulled the chair out from under an underprivileged child—a child that didn't have many friends because of her family's status among the "social classes" of Harrisburg, Illinois. After seeing how others were treated, Jonna's unfailing love for school and peers had started to diminish.

"Momma, Jesus isn't like that. Jesus has got to be mad at those kids," Jonna told me through her tear-stained face. "Didn't he say to treat others like we want to be treated? Well, that girl who pulled out the chair should be treated like that, too."

It was at that very moment I felt that she was more special than I even fully knew. It was then that I understood just how deeply she cared for others. It was then that I realized that the tummyaches were caused by an unlimited amount of compassion. It was then that I remembered hearing the words, "She is your baby, but she is my child."

Scripture says, "Finally, all of you be of one mind, having compassion for one another; love as brothers, be tenderhearted, be courteous" (1 Peter 3:8 KJV).

Perhaps she was instilled with something that I couldn't even begin to fathom. Perhaps that mystery would be unveiled over time. Just as Jesus' mother Mary, I added this to the collection of mental memories and I "pondered them in my heart" (Luke 2:19).

Chapter Six

Powerful Beyond Measure

WELL, JONNA'S JUNIOR HIGH years came and went speedily. Nothing much changed for my baby, the upset stomachs, tears, and a tremendous lack of understanding on the ways of the world remained within her. However, there was a momentous turnaround that definitely rekindled her joy.

Just prior to her junior high years, Jonna's third-, fourth-, fifth-, and sixth-grade summers, she asked if she could play softball in the girls' summer league softball program in Harrisburg.

I was happy for her to. In fact, having played all my grade school summers when I was a child and having a dad that understood the sport as my very own coach, I decided that I, too, would become a little girls' softball coach. Needless to say, my little one was on my team for all of those years. I taught her what I knew, her brother assisted, her daddy did also, as someone who had always played baseball and even once tried out for a major-league baseball team (The only reason he was turned down was because he couldn't hit a curve ball). He became a big part of Jonna's understanding for the game. It was soon evident that not only did she have the desire and the ability to play, she developed a keen understanding of the mentality needed to excel in such a competitive setting.

In the spring of her seventh-grade year, she tried out for the Harrisburg Junior High softball team and made the team. Not only did she make the team, she was one of two seventh-graders that were placed on the starting line amidst the more experienced eighth-graders.

Her dad and I were extremely proud, but it did cause some hard feelings among some of the other players. The seventh-grade girls who sat the bench were jealous, and the eighth-grade girls who sat the bench were furious. But, my little girl was on the starting lineup, and that was that! By the end of her eighth-grade year, she was a role model for the other teammates.

That season soon passed and junior high graduation was over. There were a lot of changes over that summer. I could no longer substitute in Harrisburg schools because I landed my first full-time teaching position.

I was to teach K–12 music in the little school district of Crab Orchard, Illinois. The Shackleford family moved from our little house in town to a country house eight miles south. Danny still lived in his great-grandma's downstairs apartment and was working as a diesel equipment operator. All was good, and we felt blessed beyond measure.

Then, not long before school started, Jonna approached me with what might have been the most life-changing question she could have asked at that time. She asked me if she could leave Harrisburg schools and attend high school with me at Crab Orchard. I took it to Jon, and after not much discussion, we agreed that it was a wonderful idea. She would be attending a smaller school, more individualized teaching (not that she needed it), different attitudes, and a whole new dynamic, as it was a country school. I went to Harrisburg High School, retrieved her records, told them she would not be attending, and that I invoked the reciprocity agreement between the two school districts for the sake of state funding.

Things improved vastly. My grown-up Jonna was going to start a new chapter in her life, alongside her mother. The both of us were so excited. However, starting her freshman year, we soon found out that the Lord was going to take her down a path that she was not really prepared for. Beginning that year and continuing through her senior year, he was going to show her things unimaginable to her and to use her for his glory in ways that none of us ever expected.

As you read further, I ask a favor of you, my informed readers. Please keep in mind that God *is* supernatural. He is never to be placed in a little box where he is only allowed to do things that the human mind can comprehend. Our Father, the Lord Jesus, and the Holy Spirit are more powerful than words can say. They truly are supernatural beyond measure, as I have come to discover for myself.

Please note that I am only writing the words the Holy Spirit has put into my fingers, not my mind. Each time I have sat down to write, I have started *only* after the anointment of the Holy Spirit. Yes, I know when that unction is present. Yes, I understand when the voice of the Holy Spirit, through the Lord Jesus says, "Okay, start."

The rest of Jonna's story, written through her mother, takes on the footprints of the road our Father paved for her. I give him all praise, glory, and honor for this story. I give him all the thankfulness within me for the blessing, privilege, and honor to have been chosen to be the momma of my little angel.

In other words, it is my prayer that the continuation of my writings will be either an inspiration to those who accept it as truth, an invitation of Jesus to those who don't know him to be Lord and Savior, or both.

Having said that, I will reveal the rest of Jonna's story.

Chapter Seven

Hungry for His Presence

SHORTLY AFTER OUR MOVE to the country that year, our lives took a step further along the Lord's preconceived steps for us. Jonna and I had driven in town to attend church services at the church where I grew up and she was baptized. Something happened during service that morning that sickened both of us, a thing I will not go into detail about. On the drive back home, we made the unanimous decision that neither would attend that church again. Very negative vibes were felt by both of us, leaving it unclear as to where we should go.

Just a week or two later, Jon and I decided to go to a little restaurant that we pass every day on our way to town and back. This was highly unusual for us, because Jon's idea of eating out was conveniently ordering at a drive-thru window and taking our meal home. It was a welcome surprise, though. As we walked into the door of the dining room, a precious Christian woman Jon and I both knew from years past greeted us. It was a blessing, because in my opinion, I knew of no woman except my grandma Nanny that was more of a true saint of the Lord. Jon and I ate our dinner, and while paying the bill, she asked us to come to her church for a visit. What a surprise to have Jonna's and my prayer for a new church answered in a most unexpected place and time! It was a small country church just ten miles from where we were living. She told us that there was love there for each other, and especially for Jesus. My heart jumped for joy to have acquired such knowledge. I couldn't wait to get home and tell Jonna the news, for I felt in my spirit that truly was the answer to our prayer. The Lord had surely shown me where Jonna and I were to attend church.

We found the pastor there full of the Holy Spirit, the people hungry for his presence, and they welcomed the gifts of the Spirit as the Lord deemed fit. You see, even though I was raised Southern Baptist, at the age of nineteen, I was deeply baptized with the Holy Spirit. I didn't even know what speaking in tongues was or meant simply because such expressive gifts were not allowed in the church I grew up in. I suppose it would be fair to say that it was only after my baptism of the Spirit that I discovered what this blessed gift encompassed. It was then that I knew that the gifts of the Spirit did *not* leave this world when John, the last original apostle of Jesus, went to be with him. It was that night that I realized the forcefulness of the words that John the Baptist said as he told those who had gathered at the Jordon River that Jesus would "baptize them with the Holy Spirit and fire" (Matthew 3:11). That word "fire!" The anointing of the Holy Spirit can be described as "fire." With it comes a forcefulness and fervent warmth that fire contains. Needless to say, I was overjoyed that my Lord Jesus had directed me to this church! Jonna soon attended with me, and fell in love with the people, pastor, the atmosphere, and the overall praise they shared for Jesus.

You may be asking yourself, why am I sharing this? Just wait and see. Everything I have written so far connects the dots to the purpose and meaning of my story. Did you ever connect the dots when you were little to make an entire picture? Every little detail connects to another little detail, all until it forms a grand picture. I have always heard that "hindsight is better than foresight," so I am connecting the dots for you . . . one by one.

Chapter Eight

The New School

MY DAUGHTER'S LIFE WAS set for a while . . . a new house, a new school, and a new church in our midst. At fourteen years old, what more could a girl want, right? School started late in August that year, and though she was nervous, I remember her words as she got out of the car that morning. With determination and a smile, Jonna told me, "Momma, if I need help, I know where you are." Suddenly I realized how very happy and satisfying it was knowing that your baby was right there with you all day. Not having to wonder about how she's doing in school or what she's eating for lunch revealed that a big stressor had been lifted from my shoulders. I left her outside of her first-period class feeling very satisfied that even though Jonna was now in high school, Momma was still standing by to protect and guide her throughout her days at school. "Lord Jesus, I thank you for the opportunity to have my Jonna here with me during her high school years. Now, please walk down these hallways with her and guide her in choosing new friends and in the choices she will make throughout this time. Please help her to be strong in you and to let your light shine," was my prayer as I slowly proceeded down the stairway and made the left turn onto the hallway that led to the music room of the high school. Now with my prayer being said and my daughter in her first-period class, it was my turn to prepare for my first class of the school year.

I had been worrying that my status as teacher there would hurt her chances of making friends. You know, typical stereotype "teacher's kid" stuff. There is always a common misbelief that the teacher's kid is supposed to be smart, cocky, stuck-up, and catered to by other teachers. I didn't want her getting a bad start with an unfair label. I sincerely worried that some of the country kids would have the harmful attitudes that city kids tend to carry on their shoulders, and I quickly found that, for the most part, they did not. However, I have found that in any school setting, there is always a small group so very fixed in their attitudes that they refuse to give fellow students a chance. But the strong determination born and bred into my daughter would quickly take care of that small and isolated group. I knew that she would either win them over with her Christ-like character or else she would leave them alone. I would calm myself with the belief that this little school housed students that would not, for the most part, bring back tummyaches and tears.

Jonna soon settled in with Christian friends she had made, and those students accepted her boldness in the Lord. They shared her beliefs, morals, and compassion. These students understood her and loved her for who she was and who she stood for. Among her newfound friends were those who, like my little earthbound angel, had the stamina, courage, and strength in the Lord Jesus to withstand any critical accusations or humiliating jokes that could possibly come from others who dared not to let their faith show or who chose not to have any relationship with Jesus at all. Jonna joined her friends as they prayed at their lockers, carried their well-read Bibles with them all day, freely talked about the Lord Jesus, and disregarded the snide remarks made by ignorant students who thought their religion was a joke. Not only did she join them, she joined them with a sense of belonging and a humble sense of pride that she had finally found somewhere that she felt accepted and with people that she felt accepted her. I continually gave Jesus all my praise and thankfulness because I believed his plan to be perfect both in wisdom and timing.

Yes, the Lord had surely opened a door to place Jonna Christine Shackleford in an environment that encouraged her strength in Jesus. As a result of this answered prayer for my baby girl, I found that I had received some of the greatest blessings that this momma would forever cherish deep within her heart! Giggling teenage girls infiltrated my classroom on a regular basis while down-home country "redneck" boys (and I say that with a sincere love for each and every one of them) made it a habit to stick their heads in the door and say, "Hi, Mom!" The freshman class had not only become my adopted kids, they had adopted Jonna into the ranks at Crab Orchard High School. Finally, the tears ceased, her stomachaches diminished, true friends were cultivated, and Jonna considered this small country school to be her home.

There was a slight setback the spring of that year, though. Because of an Illinois State High School Association rule, Jonna was not allowed to try out for the girls' softball team that year, because she had not attended the school for an entire year. I recall her disappointment, but I also remember the beaming smile that popped up on her face.

"It's okay, Momma," Jonna said. "It's a dumb rule, but just wait 'til next year."

That's what she did . . . she patiently waited, practiced at batting cages, worked out regularly, and became physically stronger than ever.

Chapter Nine

The Gift of Tongues

WHILE WAITING FOR THE spring of her sophomore year, that interval of time brought many blessings from the Lord. The first semester of Jonna's second year of high school brought with it an event *all* children wait for. Jonna was enrolled in driver's education. The first part, of course, was the standard classroom training and completion of her driver's test. All went well, as Jonna already knew how to drive, since we allowed her small trips down the country roads to prepare her. After passing the written test, the first anticipated event was here . . . she received her driving permit. Even though she had to drive alongside a licensed driver for twenty-four driving hours (as best as I can remember), it was an easy task for her to accomplish.

We lived twenty-five miles from Crab Orchard, and I always sat in the passenger seat while my near-sixteen-year-old committed herself to focusing on the highway traffic, changing lanes, four-way stops, and those pesky drivers who don't pay attention to anything. Before we knew it, she watched me sign the paper saying that she had driven the prescribed time with me. January 29 came and my baby girl was now sixteen years old. The 29th arrived on a Saturday that year, and before the driver's license facility opened, we were eagerly on our way to town. Since we were the first ones in line at 9:10 a.m. sharp, Jonna nestled in the driver's seat, the driving instructor (who was a cousin by marriage) was ready for the test with pen in hand, and Momma was seated in the hard aluminum chair back in the waiting room of the driver's license office. Nearly twenty minutes later, I saw my red Grand Am pull in the parking lot and my beaming daughter trying to restrain her happiness as she nearly ran into the room. "Momma, I passed. I got my license," she informed me with so much pride. I remember saying a silent prayer for the Lord to protect her and send his angels to drive with her. Needless to say, she got to drive home.

Soon after she received her license, Jon handed her the keys to his red Dodge pickup. At sixteen she finally had her license and her own truck, what could be better? Monday morning, I was all prepared to make my daily trip to Crab Orchard. I just assumed Jonna would go with me as always, since there was no use in taking an additional vehicle and riding separate. In the mind of a momma, that logic made sense. But my assumption was grossly wrong.

Jonna informed me that she was driving herself. Oh my! How my heart skipped a beat. Just as we were ready to walk out of the door to make the trip, I decided I wanted Jonna to go first so I could follow behind for safety. I proceeded to tell her that I had forgotten something and to go ahead. I stayed in the house until she backed out of the driveway, watched her pull onto the highway beside our house, and once again said, "Lord Jesus, please let your angels go with my baby. Please protect her from harm." After muttering that prayer to my Lord through tears, I left for school. All mommas reading this passage will truly understand the way my heart felt. I don't know if I was crying because I was afraid for her, or if it was the simple realization that she wasn't a baby anymore. It really didn't matter to me because, either way, I just felt like crying. By the way, she got to school fine. All was well, and I was blessed!

Jonna's driving improved as she spent a lot of time driving to and from school and visiting her friends. Some of her friends had gradually become spiritual sisters, prayer partners, and sisters in Christ. The girls would spend their time together talking, laughing, and praying. Jonna would occasionally drive to their house, stay all night with them, and attend church services on Sunday. It wasn't long after that she called me into her bedroom, asked me to sit down and talk. The words out of her mouth didn't shock me, but I wasn't expecting them.

"Momma, do you have to speak in tongues to go to heaven?" she asked.

We had never talked about this gift of the Spirit before. I didn't feel led to discuss it with her, until now.

I proceeded to tell her that this gift was not necessary to enter heaven, but that it was a wonderfully precious gift, because if used correctly, it is a language only between you and the Lord. I informed her that I had received the gift of tongues when I was nineteen years old and was extremely thankful for it. She told me that some of the kids at her friends'

church said speaking in tongues was a requirement to go to heaven because it was proof of salvation. Well, for several minutes, we discussed the
topic of speaking in tongues. She came to the conclusion that I was right,
and that it wasn't a pre-requisite for entering heaven and had nothing
to do with salvation. It was what it was—a gift from the Lord to help his
children pray. That was that!

Soon after the discussion, she was asked to attend a lock-in at the
church in Marion, Illinois. She was a little concerned that the kids would
try to pressure her over speaking in tongues again, but she was ready
with her response, "I do not have to speak in tongues to get to heaven,"
and she had planned her strategy for attack just in case anybody chose to
confront her with this belief. Well, we all know what happens when we
get too big-headed and full of pride. The result is the Lord will bring us
to our knees and just show us a thing or two. Either that, or he will let us
know that he's the King and that, indeed, his plan is perfect!

The day after the lock-in, she burst into the kitchen with the greatest news since she was saved. She had received the baptism of the Holy
Ghost, and she now could speak in tongues. I asked her if the kids had
pressured her or convinced her that she needed to. "No, Momma," she replied confidently. "It was awesome. Nobody prayed with me, and I didn't
ask the Lord to give it to me. I was praying and all of a sudden I started
praying in words I didn't understand. I was praying in tongues, and I felt
the Holy Spirit go into me, and all I could do was cry and pray. Momma,
I am so happy!" Just to put this happiness into some kind or perspective,
if possible, I would not hesitate to say that the word "happy" couldn't
possibly touch the level of emotion Jonna was feeling at that moment.
Furthermore, I can't find the words to begin to tell you the level of joy she
was on. I understand it, but only because I have experienced it.

After hearing such words, I grabbed her, held her in my arms, and
we both cried tears of delight because of Jonna's experience with the Holy
Spirit. Once again, while holding my baby girl, I heard the voice of the
Lord say, "She is your baby, but she is *my* child." Jonna didn't hear it,
because the words were meant for me. Once again like Mary, the Mother
of Jesus, I pondered these words deeply within my heart.

Finally, late winter came and softball tryouts arrived. Even after a
year of not playing softball, my athlete made the team. She was placed
on third base, the position she had played in junior high. She excelled in
this position because her fielding was outstanding, her agility was almost
unique, and she had a throwing arm that easily took the ball from third

base to first base before any runner. She loved the coach and her fellow team members.

That particular year, most of the players were returning juniors and seniors. Most of the underclass team sat on the bench, but not my girl. She quickly formed a bond with a couple of the senior girls. In other words, she earned their respect as a team member, because that's what she was. She never thought of herself as a better athlete than the other girls, but she had a confidence that mirrored a professional player. Even through the confidence, however, she displayed a humbleness that only the coach and older players could see. If you remember, I spoke of a small group of girls that resented Jonna and everything about her. The softball team brought both joy and heartache for my baby, because the simple facts that she was playing and the team was winning brought extreme happiness. The girls who continued to try to humiliate her were also on the team sitting on the bench. This added fuel to the fire, but Jonna never retaliated in any regard. She "turned the other cheek," and ignored their negativity. She didn't understand their behavior toward her, but she didn't let them bring her down to their level regardless. She stood tall (even though she was only about five-foot-two) and proud that she acted how she felt Jesus would want her to. When the softball season was over, the girls' softball team of Crab Orchard High School had gone to playoffs, only to be beaten in the last game—a bittersweet ending to a superb season. A wonderful ending to a wonderful school year.

I often asked myself, What kind of blessings would the Lord send to my baby now that she was going to be an upperclassman, a junior?

I thought about it, and in faith I knew the next year would be even better for her. I knew the next year would bring even greater things in her life unto her path. I knew the future of this precious child . . . my baby, the Lord's child, was already written down by the hand of God, the perfect plan of Jesus.

Chapter Ten

Her Journey

As the remainder of my text is the backbone of my story, I have had to wait a little while before digging into it. I awoke this morning, hearing the voice of the Holy Spirit telling me that today was the day to continue writing. You see, I am trusting the Lord Jesus will direct my fingers as I type. I stand on a firm foundation of faith, the kind of faith Abraham displayed to God when asked to pack up, leave the home he had always known, and move elsewhere. Abraham had no clue as to where the Father was leading him. He had no idea where the path Yahweh had etched into Abraham's travels would lead. However, Abraham drew in a deep breath, a gigantic step of faith, packed up and left his homeland of Ur.

"By faith, Abraham, when he was called to go out into a place, which he should after receive for an inheritance, obeyed; and he went out, not knowing whither he went. By faith he sojourned in the land of promise, as in a strange country, dwelling in tabernacles with Isaac and Jacob the heirs with him of the same promise. For he looked for a city which hath foundations, whose builder and maker is God" (Hebrews 11:8–10).

Now for some of us, that would definitely take faith at least the size of a mustard seed. But Abraham acted on his faith. Would you do what Abraham did if the Lord asked you to?

Hebrews 11:1 says, "Now faith is the substance of things hoped for, the evidence of things not seen." This kind of faith . . . believing and loving someone (God) that can't be seen is a tremendous thing to ask of mere humans. Our mind simply isn't geared to *not* be logical. However, when we accept Jesus as our Savior, he sends the Holy Spirit to live in our heart, not within our mind. The Holy Spirit isn't logical; he is spiritual.

If we trust in him as our intercessor to our Lord Jesus, we are able to see through Spiritual eyes those things that don't register in our brains.

I found an old medieval quote that I would like to share with you. Actually, I had written it on a page in an old Bible and the Holy Spirit directed me to that page this very morning.

"God does nothing, nor suffers to be done, anything but what we would ourselves, if we could see through all events of things as well as he."

These are the words that I would ask you to keep in mind as I continue with Jonna's journey.

Chapter Eleven:

Acting Upon Faith

DECEMBER 31, 1999, GAVE way to many concerns around the world. Because it was the turn of the century, many false prophets predicted the world would come to an end. Groups of people all around the world gathered on mountaintops to wait for the return of our Lord Jesus, giving no heed as to the Words of the Lord when he told the apostles, "But of that day and hour knoweth no man, no, not the angels of heaven, but my Father only"(Matthew 24:36).

I remember that so-called intelligent men of the world even declared that the entire computer system would be affected because of the New Year. In other words, all communication, business, national security, etc., would completely be wiped out. They called it Y2K.

Being a person of no superstition and knowing that nothing was going to happen unless my Father permitted it, I was not in the least concerned. Actually, I was so unconcerned that when Jonna asked me if she could go to a friend's house for New Year's Eve, I allowed her to with no reservations. But, as I watched her drive down the highway, I did utter my motherly prayer for the Lord to let his angels drive with her.

Danny had finished his degree in diesel mechanic administration and had moved back from Laramie, Wyoming, to his great-grandmother's basement apartment. He was getting ready to marry a young woman he met in Laramie and move back to Wyoming. But, that night, December 31, 1999, I knew he was home in Harrisburg. I knew Jonna was safe at her friend's house, and I knew that the Lord Jesus was in charge of anything that might come my way. As a result of this knowledge, I climbed under the covers of my warm bed along with three cats and my husband . . . and slept peacefully.

Needless to say, January 1, 2000, arrived and went with no issues. The satellite world had no meltdown, aliens didn't attack the world, and our heavenly Father chose not to send Jesus back to the earth. It was a typical New Year's Day. Parades and football were watched on television. Cornbread, fried potatoes, and beans were on the table for supper. It snowed a little outside. There were no surprises for the Shackleford family that day. Hallelujah!

Sometimes a family just needs a restful day.

Later on that month, however, there was a big surprise, one that Jonna and I had been praying for. We had faith (focus on this word again) that it would happen, and on January 20, 2000, the hoped-for present came!

There was a revival scheduled at our church that night, and Jonna had invited some of her friends from school to meet at our house and go with us. Prior to the appointed time to leave for church, Jon announced that he would go with us. I smiled at Jonna, she smiled back, and we both mouthed the words, "Thank you, Lord Jesus." When everyone had assembled at 35 Spring Valley Road, the caravan left. If I am not mistaken, our train of cars totaled five.

The evangelist that night was from Tennessee. I had been told that he was truly a "man of God," but I decided to come to my own conclusion after I met him. The message he gave was awesome! I still recall when he spoke on El Shaddai. Now, there was a name that I had never heard before. I didn't know until that message that our Father even had a name other than God. It was that night that I figured out that our Father's name wasn't God. The term "God" really is the generic, if you will, term for the Godhead—the Father, Son, and Holy Spirit. I soon realized that my Father has many names, with El Shaddai being his title when addressing him as God Almighty. However, as much I enjoyed the message given by the evangelist that night, it was no match for the thankfulness I felt for the events that soon followed.

During the closing or invitation, Jonna and most of her friends went down to the altar for a blessing from the Lord and for prayer. I soon followed because I heard the voice of the Lord ask me to go. As I was walking down the aisle, the evangelist met me before I ever got to the altar. He placed his hands on my shoulders, and we prayed together. After the "amen," I opened my eyes, and this Spirit-filled man stood silently in front of me with his eyes still closed. I knew that he was listening to the voice of the Lord. In just a few moments, he opened his eyes and revealed the message the Lord had given him.

But let me backtrack just a minute. Before I tell you what he said, I want to tell you that I had a huge problem. In the course of my lifetime, with maybe the exception of my daddy's death, this was the biggest mountain that I had ever been faced with. I didn't like it very much when my son decided to go all the way to Wyoming for college. For almost two years, I questioned the Lord's motives on that one. After graduation, my questions vanished because my baby was coming home. *But!* On the night of January 20, I was an emotional mess inside, because my baby was taking his soon-to-be wife and coming grandbaby and moving *back* to Wyoming. This time, for good!

I hadn't done a very good job hiding my grief, nor did I want to be consoled by Jon or Jonna. I found no happiness in the fact my first-born baby boy was moving 1,300 miles away. So, on that particular night, the night my little "tribe" of kids, my husband, and I attended a revival meeting, the Lord Jesus took time to reassure me that he would take care of Danny. After the evangelist from Tennessee whom I had never talked to before opened his eyes, he spoke these words: "The Lord Jesus wants you to know that he will never let go of your son."

Well, let me tell you, the tears poured from my eyes and trickled down my face. Jesus knew my heart, he knew my fears, and he loved me enough to make sure I heard these words from him. By the way, twenty-one years later, Danny, my daughter-in-law, and three grandsons still live out west; however, they now live in Spearfish, South Dakota. Furthermore, the Lord has not gone back on his word. You see, the word of the Lord is his promise. He made me a promise that night which he has never and will never break. In short, I continue to have faith at least the size of a mustard seed.

Then, dynamite went off! Just as I was trying to get my tears of relief and thanksgiving under control, Jonna came to me, hugged me, and pointed up the aisle. As my eyes glanced toward the back of the church building, tears not only started pouring out of my already-swollen red eyes again, it seemed that the tears had turned into rivers flowing from the tiny little tear ducts the Lord created in me.

"Jesus told me this was gonna happen!" Jonna rejoiced as she squeezed my hand.

Together we watched as my husband and her dad had left the back of the church and walked down the aisle. He prayed with the evangelist and our pastor. For the first time, Jon sincerely accepted the Lord as his Savior. My husband had become my brother in Christ. My joy overflowed. Soon, the tears Jonna and I shed were replaced by laughter.

If you have ever been slain by the Spirit, you understand.

Jon was touched by the hand of the evangelist, and he went out in spirit. It became a sort of game to observe, because no sooner than my born-again husband would get his "wits" back, the anointed man of God would touch Jon and out he would go again. We understood the anointing, we knew the power of the Holy Spirit, and we were watching this power at work, marking this as a truly blessed night. It was truly a night of miracles!

The next two weeks progressed, and Jonna and I often discussed the possibility that the Holy Spirit would baptize Jon with the "fire" that Luke talks about in Acts 2:1. We both understood that this kind of baptism was not necessary to enter the kingdom of heaven, for the only thing necessary is the Salvation which we receive from our Lord Jesus. Jonna admitted to me that she knew her daddy would receive it.

One night while sitting on her bed for our nightly talk, she gazed at me sternly with her big, chocolate-brown eyes, and said, "Momma, Daddy will receive it whether he wants to or not, because he will need it."

Assuming she was talking about his work the Lord would call him to do, I agreed, and the subject transitioned to something else, but I will never forget the look in her eyes. A penetrating look that I had never seen in them before. I realized that Jon wasn't the only one growing in the Lord, and that my little girl was maturing quickly in her Spiritual walk. I felt at that time that she was far more advanced in the ways of the Lord than I probably would ever be. I felt such peace knowing that she was certainly going to have a calling from the Lord, and that calling on her life would be *unreal*! Aside from that, we were in total agreement that since both of us had received the gifts of the Holy Spirit, it would be awesome if Jon did as well.

During these two weeks, we would often laugh behind closed doors. Jon would walk around the house telling the Lord that he didn't want any part of the Holy Spirit's baptism. He didn't need to speak in tongues or display any gifts of the Spirit. He was telling the Lord "No!" while Jonna and I were convinced the Lord was laughing at his futile attempt.

On February 13, Jon and I were asked to attend a church service with friends, and eagerly went with great anticipation of the Holy Spirit, for he would be present. After the message was delivered, a man from that church, a stranger to us, approached Jon and said, "Brother, I don't know you, but the Lord has told me that if you will go to the altar, he has something for you." Those words will forever be written in the chapters of my mind, because as Jon was going to the altar, I started laughing. I knew what was about to happen. I watched as Jon went to the altar—actually, behind the altar in a corner all alone. He remained a good little bit while the rest of the congregation was praising God and enjoying the presence of the Holy Spirit. Sure enough, he was praying in the "tongues of angels" when he came out of that corner. Yep! My husband had received the baptism of the Holy Spirit. Needless to say, I could not wait to get home and tell Jonna and see how excited she would be! Because she was staying all night with a friend, my news would have to wait until the next day. The next morning when I heard her truck pull into the driveway, I rushed out the door to meet her. I wanted to tell her before her daddy shared his news. At that moment, before I could get the words out, she met me with a gigantic smile and from the midst of it.

"Momma, I know! Isn't God awesome?" she spoke. "How did Dad take it?"

I ask myself to this day, How did she already know? How could she have known?

There was only one way possible. The Lord told her. This was the only logical answer. Later, she revealed to me that she had seen it in a dream the same night. Wow! Once again, like Jesus' momma, I just pondered it in my heart.

Routinely, her junior year of high school progressed, but there were some notable changes in her young life. Not long after school started that year, Jonna decided she wanted to have a part-time job. She had a few interviews at different places in Harrisburg, but she didn't feel that the Lord was leading her to work at any of them. One day, she came home from school with the news that they were hiring at the local feed store in Marion. She was given the phone number of the person in charge of hiring, so she called the number to get an interview time. I will never forget how she hung the phone up, looked at me, and said, "Momma, this is where the Lord wants me."

The next day, after school, the interview for her prospective job took place. The next day, after the interview, Jonna was hired. She came home with her red Rural King shirt telling me that she was going to start the next day. Well, I wasn't too keen on the idea. Even though her new job was only about ten miles away from Crab Orchard School, it was twenty-five miles away from our house at Spring Valley Road. I tried to convince her that a job closer to home would be more convenient, but my words went in one ear and out of the other. She said she didn't care because that's where the Lord wanted her to work.

How could I argue? There would be no point in it. I knew my Jonna and her dedication to the Lord's will for her life. So, despite my effort, after school the next day, Jonna drove to Rural King for her first day of employment.

It was like any job. For the first several weeks, she loved it. She enjoyed meeting new people and helping them with whatever they required. After time passed, the manager of the store decided to change her job from shelf-stocker to cashier. She really appreciated the change, the raise in pay, and anticipated the blessings ahead.

"Huh? Blessings?" I wondered quietly. "What blessings could she possibly be talking about? What could a cashier do for the Lord?"

Surely she wasn't going to talk to people who went through her line about him, because she would be fired for that. I knew that even in the year 2000, things were starting to change in the world, and it had become politically incorrect to talk much about Jesus in public. "Oh, well," I said to myself. She will be fine, and Jesus will take care of her.

Was I surprised to find out that that was exactly what she did? Was I surprised to find out that she never was reprimanded for it? Was I surprised to find out that many people, people I will never know, appreciated her faith, boldness, and love for the Lord? In just one word . . . no.

I was once again shown that my Jonna and my Jesus had a relationship that was indestructible. They were inseparable, but isn't that the way it was supposed to be? Jesus had chosen my little girl to be his friend, helper, and messenger. I was so honored that he chose me to be her momma.

Their partnership continued to grow. Jonna grew in Spiritual strength, Spiritual boldness, and Spiritual gifts. I have already written that she received the gift of tongues to help her in her prayer life. I have already conveyed that she had been given dreams from the Lord. I have already shown you that she was given prophecies (knowledge of things to come and messages from Jesus to tell others). During this school year, I saw Jonna completely live by the saying, "What would Jesus do?" However, she was not meek and passive. Far from it, actually. She had an unbridled spirit within her that she deliberately intended to use for the glory of the Lord. She was fearless!

I remember one afternoon early that spring. Somehow, my junior high school choir talked me into going outside instead of rehearsing that afternoon. So, instead of singing, we traveled out to the playground to play. I was sitting in a swing watching the activities of the choir and noticed that the girls' high school P. E. class had also decided to hold class outside. Jonna and a friend walked toward me and sat in the swings beside me. I inquired why they were not dressed for P. E., and Jonna spoke up to tell me they didn't feel well enough to participate. I knew that wasn't the entire truth. The honest part of the story was that they just didn't want to run around the school. They both started talking and swinging . . . in their own little world of girl talk.

If you will remember back a chapter or two, I wrote how there was a particular clique of girls who intentionally tried to hurt Jonna. Well, that afternoon, I cried as I watched Jonna reach out to one of those girls. The classmate had forgotten her tennis shoes, and she had to have them to participate in P. E. that day. Evidently, the girl was near failing in the class and couldn't afford to have any more marks for not participating. Anyway, she walked across the playground and had the nerve to ask my baby what size shoe she wore. They wore the same size. Just an hour before this event, the same classmate had laughed because the "ringleader" of these girls threw a soccer ball at Jonna. She was walking across the gym when she felt the ball hit her in the head. She looked up and realized the ball had been deliberately aimed at her. No valid reason. Simply because these girls made it their job to persecute her. The shoeless girl had the audacity to ask Jonna if she could borrow the tennis shoes on Jonna's feet. Well, my little girl, my Jonna bent forward out of the swing, untied her shoes, and handed them over. I overheard Jonna's friend in the swing beside her say, "Why did you do that? She hates you!" The reply was simple. Jonna stated, "Because Jesus would have done the same thing."

Enough said. The conversation was finished.

At the end of the day, however, this act of kindness was quickly forgotten and the foxes were after the prey once again. Once again, I pondered this in my heart.

Chapter Twelve

Junior Year

LATER THAT SPRING, JONNA once again developed the occasional bellyache syndrome, and I chalked it off as nerves and stress. She was a junior in high school and on every academic scholarship team possible. The part-time job at Rural King turned into almost a full-time job as she was working at least thirty hours a week and more considering the driving time back home at night.

Then, once again, softball tryouts were at hand. By this softball season, Jonna wasn't expected to try out. It was a given that she was on the starting lineup, and her third-base position had turned into full-time catching one behind home plate. It was always my understanding that she inherited this position initially because, as I have said before, she was fearless. The starting pitcher of the team was absolutely terrific both in accuracy and speed. As a result, the faster the ball came toward home plate, the stronger it became. I knew that a "perfect pitch" had been hurled from the pitcher due to the resounding *thud* the ball made as it landed directly into the catcher's mitt. Then, in turn, if the catcher wasn't planted on solid ground, I have also seen her tumble backwards, being knocked off balance by the precision of a pitch no batter could touch. So, Jonna's team needed a catcher and my little delicate angel girl who was as dainty as a flower volunteered. I say this with all the sarcasm that a momma should say without smiling so others could see.

My little angel had grown up so fast. Sometimes, I would just watch her and marvel how my once-little baby who walked across the monkey bars in the backyard, startling everyone who saw, had grown into such a responsible, beautiful, kind, compassionate young woman. I would just smile trying to figure out which of the boys at school, if any, Jonna might settle down with. It wasn't hard for me, however. Jonna's best friend since her freshman year was still her best friend. I reckoned that they would be best friends for life. Even though he was her everything, neither one really knew it at that time.

Many evenings, he would drive to our house and the four of us would play dominoes or some kind of board or card game. Those were always fun nights that were filled with laughter and precious memories. Momma could see something in those evenings that brought out complete changes in the two teenagers that no one else could see, except maybe Daddy.

However much devotion was shared between them as "friends," Jonna had already started dating others. Nothing really serious, but a few boys crossed our doorstep. One night, Jonna had gone out on a date. While thinking they should be sitting in the movie theatre waiting to see whatever movie was showing that weekend, I heard a car pull into the driveway, looked out the window, and saw both of them walking toward the house. Curious as to why they were not at the movies, I met them at the door and Jonna was sick. As every momma probably does, I felt her forehead, and it was cool, and there was definitely no temperature.

She said her stomach was hurting so badly. I took her to the bathroom, put a cold rag on her neck and thoroughly wiped her face with the cold rag, holding her as she cried and cried. I could not figure out what went so wrong and decided that maybe she had eaten something that simply didn't set well.

Jonna went back into the family room, sat on her date's lap, and finally went to sleep. In just a little while, my grandmother called to tell me Jonna's favorite teacher, her fifth-grade teacher, was in the hospital after having a heart attack. Jonna loved this lady so very much. Even after all the years that had passed, she cared deeply for her. The teacher/student friendship was still kindled. My grandmother and the teacher's mom were best friends. As a result, they kept up with each other through all of us mommas.

I woke Jonna up and told her the news. She looked at me with her deep, glaring eyes.

"Momma, I already know," Jonna confessed.

I asked her how the pain was, and she somewhat smiled and said, "It's gone. I'm okay."

I think the whole night was enough for her date. After that, he never came back to our house and very soon quit calling her. She honestly didn't mind too much.

A few weeks later, she was invited to a party. I didn't classify it as a date, but she drove to Crab Orchard, met a male friend at his house, and he drove them to the party. I assumed everything was normal that night. Jon went on to bed, and as usual, I waited up for her to come home. Jonna was so unusually responsible for a seventeen-year-old. Considering the estimated driving time from our house to where all of her friends lived, she had no curfew and always took my cell phone with her. There were times that she would call just to let me know she was okay. Then there were many nights she would call on the way home from school, work, or friends just to talk to me while she drove home.

So, that particular night, since I had received no phone call, I just took for granted that nothing "special" was happening. Boy! Did I miss that call!

About midnight, Jonna's truck rolled into her parking spot in the driveway and she came into the house almost running. There absolutely seemed to be a glow around her that I had not seen before. I was already awake, but still half asleep. I really thought I was dreaming.

I mean, what momma sees her daughter walking through the house with a shining reflection of a light around her? Crazy, huh?

Anyway, after coming to my senses and still recognizing there was something unusual happening with my baby, I asked her what had happened at the party.

"The party stunk," she bluntly told me. "Momma, not long after we got there, almost everyone started drinking. There were people making out all through the house, and even some drugs. I didn't want to be part of it. I knew I couldn't leave because I didn't have my truck, so I just left the house. I walked a little ways and sat down under a tree to look at the sky. I started praying for my friends inside because I knew what they were doing wasn't right. Guess what happened? I thought it was just the moon, the stars, the Lord, and me out there. But, no! Momma, I opened my eyes from praying because I felt like somebody was watching me. There was an angel standing right in front of me. It scared me at first, but the angel smiled at me. Then, I wasn't afraid anymore. I don't know how long he was there. It seemed like a little bit, but he never said anything and just smiled. I had such peace inside. Finally, I heard a voice say, 'I am proud of you, my child.' Then the angel left," she continued, "Momma, it was awesome!"

What could I possibly say after that? The glow I saw around her that night was really there. My little angel had been "touched" by an angel sent from the Lord, I truly believe. That was a double wow for me. After that, we talked a little while and decided there had been enough excitement for one night and thought we should try to get some sleep.

As I was pulling the covers down to get into bed, I heard my baby girl say, "Goodnight, Momma. I love you."

"I love you," I answered back, pulling the covers up around me. I thanked Jesus for taking care of her and then went to sleep. All was well in the world that night.

Well, after the night of what I could only explain as a supernatural visitation, Jonna only seemed to get stronger and stronger in the power of the Holy Spirit and forevermore closer to the Lord Jesus. She didn't get to go to church with her daddy and me regularly because Rural King always seemed to schedule her for eight or nine hours of work on Sundays. Of course, she didn't like it, but once in a while, she would ask for a Sunday off. It seemed that they would always redo her schedule if she asked, but she didn't take advantage of it. Jonna thought that as long as she was working, maybe someone else could go to church.

As I said prior, the power of the Holy Spirit just continued growing within my child. I saw her lay hands on a sick friend at school. One day during lunch, I decided to stay in my classroom to grade some papers. I

went to the teacher's room, grabbed a Diet Coke, and went back to my room. When I opened the door, there was Jonna and a friend, which was nothing out of the ordinary. Jonna, her friends, my high school students, or any of the above often came into my room before school, at lunch, during study halls, and after school.

"Whatcha doin'?" I asked.

They informed me that they were going to have prayer because Jonna's friend had a horrible migraine and had been puking due to the pain. I just smiled and said, "Okay, do you want me to leave?"

The answer was a unanimous "No!"

I sat down at my desk, prepared my papers to be graded, and overheard Jonna praying over her friend. Silently, I was praying, too. After a little while, I started my paperwork and tuned their prayer session out. I knew Jonna, the Holy Spirit, or Jesus didn't need my help. Grinning to myself, I started making red marks on incorrect answers. I was concentrating on some of the most amusing answers I had ever seen on a music history test, and I didn't notice the girl's prayer time had ended. I felt four eyes staring down on me, looked up, and asked how it went.

I already knew the answer, though.

The young girl was healed in my room that very moment. Her nausea was gone, the dizziness had vanished, and her head had no pain at all. We all gave Jesus the glory. The girls left to go eat lunch because they said they were starving, and I tried to finish grading papers that afternoon, but never did get them done. All I could think about was how the Lord was using my little girl for his glory. I felt so proud (not in a prideful way, but a thankful way) and honored that Jesus, who knew Jonna before she was even in my womb, had selected me to be her momma.

As if school, work, studies, and social life weren't enough, softball season had begun. Jonna talked to her boss, explained that she had to schedule work around softball practice and games, and asked to be cut back to her regular part-time hours. The new scheduling was agreed on, and Jonna's catching days had begun once again.

Needless to say, her ability to control the game from behind the plate entitled her to become "captain" of the team. I knew that softball/baseball was as much mental as physical, but I underestimated how my little catcher understood the mechanics of this game. By the way, that part came from her daddy. I knew the game, as I had grown up around it, played it, coached it, and learned it. But Jon had grown up playing it and learning it, too. On top of that, Jonna's brother had grown up around baseball, played it, and was also a catcher.

I don't think she had much chance to not love it, but her ability to analyze what was going to happen next in the game was remarkable, at least to me.

The school year was over before we knew it. Jonna had a fulfilling academic year. As I said before, she was somewhat of a perfectionist and expected no less than straight As from herself. This year held true to form, except there was one little glitch. Jonna made a B in French class the last nine weeks of school. She wasn't happy and decided to talk to her teacher. The cause of the unwanted grade was a misunderstanding on some kind of project. The project was completed, but not exactly according to the teacher's specifications. The grade turned out to be legitimate and impartial. Jonna accepted it, but pouted a little bit. Yes, she definitely had some of her momma in her.

Chapter Thirteen

My Musical Prodigy

As I SIT DOWN to write this morning, I have many memories running through my mind. You see, it's my birthday. Birthdays come and go—birthdays are just another day on the calendar. At least that's the way I see it. Though I am not really thinking about my past birthdays, I am sitting pondering about Danny and Jonna's past ones. In 2021, my little boy turned forty-three and Jonna turned thirty-eight. Wow! How time flies! My parents and grandparents told me as I grew up that the older we get, time passes more quickly. I didn't realize that they were right, until I started getting older. One day we will be on God's calendar and his time, for Scripture says that there will be no night in heaven. There will be no sun because the light of our Lord Jesus will light the way.

The summer between Jonna's junior and senior year remained pretty routine. She started taking classes at Southeastern Illinois College as it was her intention to major in child psychology. She began to have such a heartfelt burden for the little ones who were abused, more emotionally than physically (if there's a difference?). That summer, she enrolled in a psychology class, an active physical education class, and a music history class which I taught. The music history class turned out to be awesome. She, of course, aced it. But why wouldn't she? She had been my study mate all the nights at the kitchen table in our little four-room house that was used to shelve massive study notes, theory papers, compositions, and books while I was going to Southern Illinois University. Being a music major encompassed all different avenues of study. Jonna helped me prepare for almost every test in all areas of music. She learned about Beethoven, Mozart, Bach, and Brahms. While I studied for a music theory class, she was eager to understand the difference between a major/

minor 3rd and an augmented 7th. The only preparation my little musician couldn't help me with was practicing the piano. All music majors are required to declare a primary instrument for study and performance. Mine was piano since I began taking piano lessons at the age of five. Having said that, a piano major was required to give a senior recital for the public in order to graduate with a Bachelor's of Music degree. Even though she couldn't help me practice the long three to four hours every day for six and a half years, she grew to love the music of the Classical, Romantic, and Twentieth-century musical periods. Also, when I would have to go back to Carbondale, Illinois, at night to attend a required concert, most of the time she would go with me. I never knew exactly if her presence was because she loved the atmosphere of the School of Music at SIU or if it was to keep me company on the hour-long drive back home. Either way, I greatly appreciated her accompanying me.

I suppose "the acorn doesn't fall too far from the tree." Not only did she learn college-level music theory, history, and composition alongside her momma, her first interactions with music started when she was four years old. It was after her intentions to learn to play the piano had been voiced that I sat beside her on the piano bench and guided her little fingers to play songs like *Mary Had a Little Lamb* and *Twinkle Twinkle Little Star*. Along with her desire to play my piano, I noticed her ability to succeed in this art was making itself more apparent every day. It didn't take me long to notice the strength her fingers displayed and the form they held as she pushed each note on the keyboard down. Then, one afternoon, she informed me in a matter-of-fact voice that she no longer wanted to play the songs that I was trying to teach her. She wanted to play the grown-up songs that I played.

She most definitely demonstrated the ability to mentally piece the music all together. That characteristic combined with the mature mind-body coordination she had already proven to have indicated that she was ready to begin her music training on the keyboard.

There was a definite problem, however. Jonna wanted to plunge forward before Momma was ready. Soon after I began giving her actual lessons, I realized that even with my training I wanted her to be instructed by someone other than me. So I called the most accomplished, dedicated, and top-notch piano teacher that I had ever met. She graciously informed me that it wasn't common practice to start lessons before the age of seven or eight. But after discussing it for a while, I convinced her that Jonna was ready, both mentally and physically. This dear lady responded with these words:

"Christy, I know you have grown up playing the piano. I respect your decision," she told me. "We will give it a shot."

Well, that shot turned into the next eleven years of piano lessons, contests, and recitals, and I will never forget the last music contest that my daughter entered. Jonna was thirteen years old, and the selected piece wasn't easy. Keeping in complete character, Jonna decided she needed help perfecting it. Momma's help wasn't what she wanted. She informed me she needed "professional" help for the piano contest. I was still attending Southern Illinois University Carbondale at the time, and it was my senior year as a piano major. My piano professor, who had also become a very good friend, agreed to meet with us in his studio that next Saturday morning. After listening to Jonna's fingers slide across the keyboard with precision and dexterity, he offered suggestons that my budding prodigy took to heart. Within just a few weeks, the music produced by her roving fingers on the keyboard went from wonderful to exceptional. Because of my professor's suggestions and because of his expertise as a world-renowned pianist, Jonna's self-confidence as a musician escalated.

As a result, I sat and cried as she performed Mozart's *Fantasy in D minor, K. 397.* for the judges and audience the morning of the contest. The piece was perfect—no memory lapses, no shaky fingers, no forgotten musical flare-up. Only heartfelt emotion that rang pure from her fingertips to the keyboard. I knew the perfection, she knew it, the audience knew it (as they gave a standing ovation), and the judges knew it. The result—a first superior rating! After reading the comment sheets from different judges, none of them found anything wrong with her musical performance.

Needless to say, this piano-major momma was on cloud nine! It wasn't just her innate love of music that determined her love for the music history class. I have to believe that she loved the teacher . . .

. . . The devoted, loving, caring, music teacher that Jonna's first college music class was *me*! To say the least, both of us enjoyed sharing the class that summer.

Chapter Fourteen

Educational Crossover

THE SUMMER PROGRESSED, AND we received the news that the State Board of Education had ruled that students had to attend the schools in the district they lived in. Now, that was a slap in the face considering that Jonna had attended Crab Orchard High School since her freshman year and had developed friendships that were life-long. Now, her senior year, the state says she can't finish her high school years where she started.

Yes, there were a few tears shed over that one.

Of course, as all other decisions made by the State of Illinois, it was all because of funding. As unhappy as she was, off we went to Harrisburg High School and admitted her. In a way, however, she was looking at the positive side, keeping in mind that she would be graduating with the kids that she started kindergarten with. At least that was how she was trying to justify anything good from this decision.

All was set. School started. Once again, she arrived home unhappy and unsettled. I was worried about her. I mean, what student should have to be taken away from high school teachers, friends, and lifelong memories just before graduation? In my opinion, it just wasn't fair. I decided to talk to my principal about it, and she informed me that there were exceptions to all rules. If Harrisburg High School would sign a waiver releasing their funding to Crab Orchard School, Jonna could finish and graduate from her alma mater. I was so excited to hear it.

After Jonna got home from school that day, as she was getting ready to drive to Marion to work, I shared the news with her. Because I didn't raise my children to be quitters, she said that she would stick it out. It wasn't all that bad, because she could leave at noon and still be able to drive to Rural King without having to hurry. I was surprised in her decision, but supported her fully. In a way, I was relieved, because she could go to work earlier, work her shift, and would arrive home earlier at night.

But the surprise of all surprises came about a week later. I was called to the office to answer a phone call one morning, and couldn't imagine it being anything but bad news. Everyone knew I was working. When I got to the office, the secretary was smiling and informed me that it was Jonna.

"What's wrong, baby?" I answered the phone worriedly. Knowing I had also raised my children to not be afraid to talk to others, not to be afraid to confront an issue, and not to be afraid to stand up for what they believed in, my daughter told me in a determined, matter-of-fact voice, "Momma! I can't take this anymore. I want to come back to Crab Orchard."

Well, it just so happened that my principal was standing in the door. I relayed the message and asked her if Jonna could come back. I truly think some students have advantages with teachers/principals. Being a teacher, I don't believe that it's always because they are a "teacher's kid," have a socially well-known last name, or are an all-star athlete. I was always resisting the urge to show partiality to some students, but it was the students who earned my respect. Overall, well-rounded students who demonstrated a solid and trustworthy character were the first to have any special privileges. Jonna's graduating class had a few of those students mingled in the large class of forty-something.

"Tell her to come on," the principal told us. I truly believe that because she had earned the respect of all administration and faculty there, our principal did not hesitate. I relayed that message to Jonna. She was to go to the principal, turn in her books, and inform them she had my permission to withdraw from Harrisburg High School. I added that if they had any questions, to call me.

"I already have," Jonna said. "I turned in everything, signed myself out, and explained that I wouldn't be back. After that, I told them that whatever paperwork they needed, Crab Orchard would send them."

Yep, that was my girl.

Within thirty minutes, I heard my classroom door open and saw my content little girl bouncing through the door.

"Hi, everybody!!" she beamed. "Just wanted to let you know I was here, Momma! Goin' to the office to sign in. Oh, by the way, I knew I was comin' back. That's why I did it all myself."

I asked her just how she knew without even asking. Smiling, she just said, "The Lord told me. See ya later!"

Later that day, during lunch hour, my heart rejoiced inside when I looked over at the kids eating lunch, and there sat my daughter in her spot at the lunch table with her friends. The small group of girls, the ones who had been to slumber parties, game nights, and nights just because were laughing, giggling, and smiling—just as it had been for the past three years.

"Thank you, Lord Jesus, for taking care of my little girl," I smiled to myself and whispered, "Thank you for your perfect plan."

Chapter Fifteen

Gift of Discernment

WHAT COULD BE MORE exciting than a child's senior year of high school? There were preparations to be made toward college credits, picking a college, making lasting memories, and turning eighteen. As a result, Jonna seemed to stay on a "natural high." Somewhere between her spiritual life and her earthly life was the world she lived in. Her passion for helping abused and neglected children grew stronger with each passing day. Because of her anticipation of the coming days, at times she seemed to be walking on clouds.

She had already received the necessary high-school requirements for graduation. Now, she was working on classes for entrance to the local junior college. We were discussing the possibilities of different colleges, as Jonna received approximately thirty-something college invitation brochures. She was invited to visit them based on her academic achievements and her ACT scores, etc. However, she decided that she would attend Southeastern Illinois College since she had already taken classes there. This was much to her dad and momma's relief. We both felt like a child grew up a lot during the junior college years. Jonna was unusually mature for her age and always had been, but the truth was I just wasn't ready to cut the apron strings. After all, she was my baby, and her brother was already gone.

Anyway, there was a class she needed for college entrance that Crab Orchard simply didn't offer. The counselor at the school advised Jonna that she could take it first in the mornings at Marion High School. Jonna was enthused about participating in a different school. She was really happy that this schedule allowed her to sleep in a little later. The new schedule started about a week after she had enrolled in Crab Orchard, and when the class at Marion was over each day, she would drive back to Crab Orchard and come to my room. There she spent the next twenty minutes or so getting ready for her first class of the day. I didn't notice anything different about her appearance for a while.

Then, one morning I noticed that she was disturbed and distraught.

Of course, I had to ask if everything was all right. She looked at me with tears in her eyes and asked if I could leave my class long enough to go into the hallway. I didn't hesitate because I was a teacher, but a mother first. She told me that since the first morning at Marion, she had developed a stomachache and nausea every morning. She didn't know why, but the symptoms passed as quickly as they started. This morning, though, it was really bad. "Momma, why do I get so sick?" she asked.

Well, I didn't know what to do.

This had been an off-and-on issue for years, but we knew that it usually only happened when she was upset. Then, the Lord brought to my memory the night she came home from a date—the night her teacher had a heart attack. I told her to ask the Lord why, and he would tell her. Sure enough, he did.

The next morning, she walked into my classroom with a bothered look on her face, but far different than the expression she had shown me the day prior. Once again, she wanted me to come to the hallway. Because my daughter needed to talk to me, I turned to my high school choir class and explained that I would just be outside the door and to keep their talking down to a low roar. She shared the details of how every morning she walked the same path through the halls of Marion High School.

She said when she started feeling ill that morning, she stopped walking when she heard the Lord's voice talking to her. He didn't waste any time showing her the students she was walking passed in the hallway. The students were dressed in goth, sporting satanic emblems on their folders, and piercings. Now, let me say before I go any further that the manner of dress did not indicate their demonic character. Goth is just a style, nothing more. However, Jonna immediately saw Satan's decals on the books/folders the students carried. She informed me that the Lord had spoken to her that it was his gift of discernment that was being fulfilled in her. In other words, the Holy Spirit living inside of Jonna could not be around the evil spirits of these students. The spirits were clashing, and Jonna was feeling the spiritual warfare going on around her. She told me that the Lord had shown her an alternate route to take to her class by walking outside the school.

The very next morning, Jonna came dancing through the doorway of my room. She had that glow around her as I had seen before. Immediately, I knew everything was okay. She didn't ask me to go to the hallway that morning. She boldly announced that the Lord was right. She had taken the outside scenic route far away from the problematic students.

"The Lord is absolutely wonderful," she said. Before I could say a word, she had turned around and nearly skipped down the hallway just like a little girl.

Realizing that my class was getting a little louder with each passing minute, I immediately turned and entered the classroom where several of the students were standing at the door trying to overhear the conversation occurring in the hallway. The junior-high class that was supposed to be practicing their choir music in my room had no idea what she was talking about. When confronted with the "silliness" Jonna was demonstrating, I simply said, "Jesus took care of a problem she was having, and she is happy." That took care of any further questions.

Later that day, I saw Jonna in the library reading her Bible instead of eating lunch. I didn't go talk to her, as I realized she was studying. However, I tucked it away in my mind for further inquiry.

With that issue addressed and resolved, Jonna was at peace with school, the job, and her "world" at the moment. I can't recall anything earth-shattering that happened that semester. Fall break came and went, leaves fell, and southern Illinois started preparing for Thanksgiving.

Chapter Sixteen

Thanksgiving

As MUCH AS JONNA loved birthdays, Easter, and Christmas, Thanksgiving Day was her favorite holiday. The feel of an autumn day, parades on television, turkey, dressing, going to Papaw Charlie's and Mamaw Mary's for dinner, and football gave her, as she always said, "a warm fuzzy feeling." She never forgot one special Thanksgiving Day when we were just about to file into Mamaw's kitchen to say the Thanksgiving blessing when the smoke alarms started going off, the house quickly filled with smoke, and everyone ran to see what was going on. Well, Mamaw Mary had forgotten the marshmallow-covered sweet potatoes in the oven.

You got it!

The marshmallows had caught on fire. As soon as the fire was put out and we realized it was nothing serious, the house became bubbling with laughter. We were still laughing as we sat down to dinner and ate Mamaw's scrumptious dinner, all but the sweet potatoes. It was a day of laughter, love, and thanksgiving. But then, that's what the day was supposed to be about, right?

Just about as soon as the Thanksgiving season came, it went, and that heralded in the Christmas season. But before I dive into the midst of that, there is something that must be written.

The Sunday after Thanksgiving was a beautiful, sunny Lord's Day. I will never forget that day. It is etched into my backlog of memories, forever! Jon and I started the day by driving to church. I loved the drive to church that time of year. The little church building sat beside Karber's Ridge Road. If you are familiar with that area of southern Illinois at all, you will know that when it is fall, it may be the most beautiful place around. The colors of the leaves, the crispness in the air, and the usual sight of deer always directed me to marveling at the creation of my Lord God!

Church service was over; we drove back to 35 Spring Valley Road, ate some dinner, and waited until church service that night. I well remember that the Holy Spirit made his awesome presence known that night during service, but that wasn't unusual. I was so caught up in his presence that I didn't notice a dear, precious, Holy Spirit-filled man of God approach me. I felt someone take my hand and proceed to lead me to the altar.

Immediately, I saw the expression in his eyes and knew something was up. I still see the stern and serious look in dreams sometimes. I can still hear the tone of his voice.

"Sister Christy, I have never been asked to do this before, but the Lord wants me to tell you that you will face a great tribulation," he said. I can still hear the tone of his voice "But, if you keep your eyes on him, you will be okay."

What could I say after that? I knew that it was indeed a message from the Lord, because I knew the reputation of this man's prophecies. I don't remember saying anything—I couldn't say anything. I gave him a hug and walked back to my seat beside Jon. Well, the rest of the service faded away. I couldn't tell you what happened in that little white building anymore that I can tell you what happened on June 11, 1960! My spirit was at peace, but my mind was in a whirl.

After the meeting was over, I told Jon what the dear brother had prophesied to me. He asked me if I had any idea what it could be. Of course, the Lord had only told me enough to let me know I needed to rely on him. The pastor was in the office as we were getting our coats on to leave. I went in and told him the words that were given to me. As he explained to me that there were many kinds of tribulations and it probably was just a little trial. As my spirit connected with the Holy Spirit once again, I realized that my Jesus didn't mean a daily, routine part of life. My Jesus loved me enough to let me know he was preparing me for a powerful tribulation. Perhaps the life-changing kind, but most assuredly not a little trial. I knew something was coming. Was is Jon? Was it Danny or Jonna? Was it illness? Surely it wasn't a death? When? Who? How? Why? NO! I can't ask why because I believe my God's plans to be perfect, or do I? Whatever the answers were to the question I had, only one thing was important at this point. I had complete faith and trust in my Lord Jesus. Whenever my "great tribulation" did arrive, I absolutely knew that my Lord was going to be there with me.

Chapter Seventeen

Perfect Wisdom

NEEDLESS TO SAY, THE human part of me tried to pry into God's business and figure out what in the world the Lord was preparing me for. Needless to say, the following days during prayer, I would ask the Lord to let me know what was going to happen, even just a glimpse or a hint. But because of his perfect wisdom, the only response I ever heard was "Keep your eyes on me. Do not turn to the left or the right."

Eventually, as I felt myself growing to a new height of spirituality, I knew that my questions to him were fruitless. I knew deep within my spirit that I simply had to trust Jesus. Gradually, the desperation to find out more faded away. I kept his words in heart, however. In other words, I never buried them deep within my soul only to be forgotten. No, Jesus wasn't going to let me forget them.

At any given moment, I would hear his voice saying, "Keep your eyes upon me!" No, my precious, loving Lord and Savior intended to make sure I remembered them. For this, I am eternally thankful!

It was during that season of my spiritual growth and trust in Jesus that Jonna received a prophecy, too. One Sunday morning while attending service in that little white building on Karber's Ridge Road, Jonna had gone to the altar to talk to Jesus.

"You will be gone for a while, but you will be back," she heard his words. As prophecy has the tendency to be spoken and not understood by human brains, she didn't understand this spoken word any more than I understood what the Lord was preparing me for. It didn't matter, though. Just hearing the voice of the Lord made her happy. Any time Jonna heard the Lord's voice, she was thankful and jubilant! She would, however, understand them in the days to come.

It's a mystery to me, but a wonderful mystery, that the human mind processes millions of tiny particles of information in a day's time, and only a tiny, tiny bit is remembered. However, right before Jesus was crucified, he told the apostles in that small upper room the night he was arrested, "If ye love me, keep my commandments. And I will pray the Father, and he shall give you another Comforter that he may abide with you forever. Even the Spirit of truth; whom the world cannot receive because it seeth Him not, neither knoweth him: but ye known him for he dwelleth with you, and shall be in you" (John 14:16–17).

My readers must understand that it is only through the presence of the Holy Spirit that we remember the words that the Lord Jesus tells us.

"But the Comforter, which is the Holy Ghost, whom the Father will send in my name, he shall teach you all things, and bring all things to your remembrance, whosoever I have said to you" (John 14:26).

You see, even though the human mind stores everything processed by it, we don't always know how to pull it out of storage to remember it. Believe me, as I get older, it is harder and harder to know the right lever to pull so I can remember anything. But because of the wisdom of the Holy Spirit, the messages that the Lord gives us don't fade away into a storage bin, the Holy Spirit knows just exactly when we need to remember them. Then, he brings them "to our remembrance."

As the leaves were definitely falling and the autumn temperatures were dropping, there was a family in our church experiencing major difficulties. Within the walls of their house, noises were heard, shadows were cast, and the woman of the house was experiencing severe mood swings, depression, and anxiety. The church had prayed with her, with her husband, and with their children but to no avail. The darkness inside the confines of the house prevailed. On a certain fall afternoon, our pastor was driving down a road praying about this desperate situation. All of a sudden, in front of his car he was shown a revelation of the unanswered mystery. The Lord revealed him the form of a demon floating outside the windshield of the car. Mind you, it wasn't a real one at that time, just a vision of one. As this demonic image was revealed, the Lord told him that one had been allowed inside of the family's house.

Jon and I received a phone call that night asking if we would be willing to go with a small group of fellow Spirit-filled Christians to exorcise the house. After discussing the possible circumstances of this task, Jon and I agreed to be part of the mission. We were to meet at our house the next night to caravan to the "infected" house. Through the power of the

Lord Jesus, we wanted to make the unwanted guest leave the premises. My heart fell as Jonna proceeded to ask me if she could be part of the team. I pushed the responsibility of answering to our pastor by telling my brave child to ask him.

I never talked to him about it, but Jonna called him immediately. His answer was very simple. He told her to pray about it the next day and see what Jesus wanted her to do. Now, why didn't I think of that? At that time, I was thinking as a momma, not a child of God.

If you have never been part of a church body which allows and practices the *fullness* of the Holy Spirit and doubts *nothing* that he or the Lord Jesus can do, I am sure that you are questioning my words at this moment. Jesus cannot be put in a little safe container that only is opened when the owner of that box believes it is necessary. Our Father, Jesus, and the Holy Spirit are totally supernatural, totally powerful, and totally God! Fact is, we either believe the power they possess, or we might as well not believe any of it.

If my readers have any knowledge of the supernatural and spiritual realm, they must admit that angels do exist and along with angels . . . demons. Yes, Satan brought one-third of the heavenly, God-created angelic force to earth with him the moment he was kicked out of heaven for pridefully thinking that he could claim the Father's place on the Godly throne.

Therefore, so became demons!

These supernatural beings are as real as you and I. Because the spiritual world is inhabited by God's good angels, it must be inhabited by Satan's evil demons. One day, soon and very soon, all evil in this world will be destroyed by Jesus and put into its rightful place, the Lake of Fire for eternity.

Anyway, that's a different story for another time. According to scripture, demons dwell in something, whether it is humans, cows, pigs, cats, frogs, or houses. In the case of this family, the demon was in their house tantalizing everyone who lived there. Demons are pretty smart creatures. They are fully aware that when they are forced to leave one place, they must find another residence. As a result, if the Christian bodies present are not prayed up, Spirit-filled, protected by the blood of Jesus, and ordained by the Lord to perform this exorcism, they best leave it to whomever the Lord calls to perform it. If not, there is a definite possibility the demon can leave the former place of residence and find a nice, warm dwelling inside of you. These supernatural displays did not stop as soon as Jesus' apostles left this earth. These occurrences are as prevalent in 2021 AD as they were in 65 AD.

(Okay, my theology lesson in the supernatural realm is over. I ask that you hear me out before rendering this story ridiculous.)

No sooner than I heard Jonna's truck roll into the gravel that filled our driveway, I heard the door shut. The patter of feet rapidly walking through the living room and stopping in Jonna's bedroom. Then, my ears heard the closing of her door. As usual, Momma was concerned that something was wrong, so I opened the door.

"What?" she looked up and said. I asked her if she was okay and I noticed the look in her eyes—A look full of . . . ? Yes, I had seen that look many times before. Those chocolate-brown eyes held a look of stern determination. A gaze from deep within which wasn't focused upon any-thing, including me. Even though she was holding a conversation with me, the spirit intensely glowing from her heart was keenly set on the business of the moment which clearly I was intruding upon. They were saying, "Momma, I am fine. Please go away because I am talking to Jesus."

As soon as I realized that I was definitely not needed in the stillness of that room, I turned and went back to the kitchen. Often fasting goes along with prayer, and we had all been fasting since the day before. As I am hypoglycemic, I felt that I should absolutely get something with carbs in my belly before we left to battle whatever it was. Jon wasn't ready to eat, but while I was getting some juice from the refrigerator I noticed feet standing beside me. I rose up to find Jonna standing there with an expres-sion on her face that only meant one thing. Jesus said no!

The Lord had told her that he wanted her to stay at our house, but to pray while we were gone. Yes, disappointment prevailed, but she knew to be obedient to the Lord Jesus.

As the members of God's army started arriving at our house on Spring Valley Road, Jonna's disappointment turned to jubilation. She knew there was a reason why she was denied the chance to battle an actual demon. She admitted that she didn't know the reason was, but was excited about whatever the plan of action was. All six of us gathered around our kitchen table, Jonna included, said a final group prayer, and left the sanctity of our house. I remember looking at my beautiful little girl and saying, "Jonna, I love you. Don't worry." She smiled and said, "I love you, too. Don't you worry."

I had peace!

Upon arriving at the "possessed" house, we were told to stay together as a group. The team walked into each room of the structure and the pastor anointed the walls with oil. Soon, the job was complete . . . After praying as one that the demon would leave, there came stillness, calmness, an undisturbed peace within all of us. The demon had left the premises. We had defeated the evil presence by the precious blood of Jesus. What a night it was.

When we drove back to Spring Valley Road, none of the others came in. They decided it had been a long but profitable night and eating supper was the next thing on the agenda. Jon and I agreed. When I unlocked the door and went in the house, Jonna was sitting on the couch with her Bible. It wasn't difficult to notice the contentment on her face. "The demon left, didn't it?" were the words spreading through the family room. I didn't understand what she was saying. I didn't catch the message that she *knew* it left. I told her that it did leave the family's house. She caught my complete attention when she spoke the next words.

"I knew it left. It came here," she said with a solemn, matter-of-fact voice.

"What do you mean?" I asked. It was at that moment that I understood why the Lord didn't want this child to attend the battle. It was at that moment that I realized the anointment the Lord had given to my baby. It was at that moment that I realized that she wasn't my baby anymore. I quietly listened as she dictated the events that she experienced at Spring Valley Road that night.

Jonna stated that as soon as we left the house, she went into her bedroom, got her Bible, and started praying for our safety and for the unwanted houseguest to be evicted. She said she began to feel an uneasiness and heaviness in her stomach. The same feeling that she experienced when she was around evil spirits. She said she went into the living room, started a fire in the fireplace, sat in front of the dancing flames to warm up, and continued talking to Jesus about what was going on not far down the highway from where she sat. She said that the Holy Spirit made his presence known to her, and she felt the uneasiness and nausea in her stomach leave. She explained that she didn't really know how long she had been praying when she heard a knocking sound against the living room window. Even though it was dark outside, the vapor light over our driveway illuminated the porch just enough that she was able to see some form of silhouette outside of the window. She said the presence

kept knocking, and she kept praying. But, she made sure that I understood that she wasn't afraid because the Lord was with her. Evidently, the
"thing" outside was insisting that she let it enter. You see, demons cannot enter into the presence of the Holy Spirit, nor occupy space already
taken up. Jonna was so very full of the Holy Spirit that there was no way
any of Satan's army could have attacked her. However, if she had opened
the door to it, the demon could have entertained the idea that she was
inviting it inside. On the other hand, if the demon would have found
that space to be unoccupied at the moment, well, it would have not-so-
politely invited itself in and would have found a new home.

Because of the obedience Jonna had shown to the Lord Jesus that
night and because of the discernment the Holy Spirit had given her, this
precious child of God knew exactly what was happening and exactly what
to do. The last step, the step to make the demon go away, was exactly what
she did. She said the harder she prayed, the more persistent the knocking became. She said it sounded like the window was coming apart at
the frame. Who really knows how long this went on because there is no
recognizable timetable when the spiritual world is concerned. But after
a bit, Jonna said the words "In the name of Jesus Christ, Lord and Savior
of all creation, I rebuke you. You have to leave." She said that she had
been praying in the Spirit all night, or praying in tongues (whatever you
want to call it), but suddenly when those words came out of her mouth,
they were clearly in bold, clear, and majestic-sounding English. Suddenly,
as quickly as the knocking started, it stopped. When she glanced at the
window, there was no more "presence" looking inside at her.

"Thank you, Jesus!" she said, laughing. "Whew! That was something!"

I guess she found the entire ordeal funny, or perhaps it was just a
big relief to her. Either way, you might have wondered why the Lord told
Jonna she had to stay home that night. He needed the faith, strength, and
boldness of his child to protect 35 Spring Valley. He required the house to
be full, not empty, when the demon caller decided to move in. Jesus used
his child (my baby) to protect his children. I thanked him for his love
and protection that night, I thanked him for taking care of my baby, and
I thank him still, twenty years later. In fact, I will continue to praise him,
thank him, and love him all the days of my life. (By the way . . . I intend
to live forever, so that's a long time.)

Even though it was a night we will never forget, we ate until we were full, went to bed, and all three of us went to sleep knowing we were safe in the arms of the Lord.

Intense, huh? Well, you haven't read anything yet. Just remember, don't ever underestimate the miraculous power of the Lord God.

Chapter Eighteen

Jonna's Mission

As THE CHRISTMAS SEASON was upon us, there was excitement at school produced by decorating the classroom, preparing for the Christmas concert, practicing for the holiday basketball tournaments, and talk of Christmas vacations. Jonna joined in with the various activities throughout the school. At this time, she was happy-go-lucky and carefree. I noticed that she was spending more time in Bible study at home and less time watching TV at night. This didn't alarm me or surprise me but I did see a change.

One evening, she announced that she had asked for the coming Sunday off because she needed to go to church with her dad and me. Great idea, I felt.

I loved sitting in the church pew with Jon on one side and my baby on the other. The only thing that would have given me more happiness was to have Danny there with us, but that wasn't possible. Wyoming was just too far for him to come to church with us. I soon found that there was a specific reason for Jonna's attendance that Sunday morning. She told me that there was an older lady whom she worked with that was really sick. She had been diagnosed with some sort of cancer. Jonna said while she was talking to the woman about Jesus and his wonderful healing power, the Holy Spirit filled her and was led to pray with the woman. After the prayer, the woman informed Jonna that she knew who Jesus was, but that she wasn't a proclaimed Christian. She had never given her life to the Lord and accepted the fact that he died for her.

My little girl, now grown into a well-rounded Christian young woman, had a mission. She was talking to Jesus about her friend, and he said to get a prayer cloth at church. For those of you who don't know the meaning of a prayer cloth, it was a plain white handkerchief (it could have been any color for that matter) which the Spirit-filled people at our church prayed over asking for the Lord to heal someone. After that, the cloth was given to the needy person to lay on whichever part of the body was sick.

After church service that morning, Jonna informed the pastor of the need, and he produced a regular white handkerchief. Jonna knew the members of our church who were truly Spirit-filled and believed in the power of the Holy Spirit. The pastor called together those brothers and sisters in Christ to pray over the cloth. You must realize that the cloth in itself had *no* power, it was the *faith* of those who prayed that bestowed the healing presence of the Lord.

Jonna fasted that night and prayed longer for the woman's healing. The next morning, she told us that she was going to visit this precious lady and that she would be a little late. I completely understood and as she was driving off, I remember giving my Lord Jesus all praise and glory for the healing that he was getting ready to give. Then, I thanked him for my baby, his child.

It wasn't too long after Jonna's shift was over that she called to tell me the news.

"I know the healing will come for her, but guess what? She was saved. She accepted Jesus as her Savior!" Jonna beamed. My angel girl had led another to Jesus. I stopped again to give thanks to my Jesus, yet once again I realized that I was a truly blessed mother. After all, I felt I had the most remarkable children in the world.

Christmas Day was knocking on our door, and Jonna was working more hours than usual due to the Christmas shopping rush. She didn't mind because the season allowed ample opportunities for her to witness to customers as they went through her checkout line. As usual, nobody ever complained that the bouncy, kind, and caring young woman at the cash register was witnessing about her Jesus. Do you suppose that was because Jesus intended for Jonna to tell others about him? For sure!

Just a few days before Christmas, Jonna called from work to tell me the news. The woman who was expected to only be on this earth for a few more months no longer had any signs of cancer! Jesus completely healed her and had done it through my angel! Wow!

What better Christmas present could anyone ask for? It was the faith of those who prayed that Sunday that caused the Lord Jesus to listen intently to the prayer that was offered to him. Yes, Jonna was his messenger because she was obedient to his voice, but Jesus received *all* the glory that day and now for the miracle he performed.

Between the blessing Jesus gave my baby girl's friend and the blessing of the celebration of Jesus' birth, it was truly a season of joy and love around our house. While Jon was working one Sunday afternoon, Jonna and I put together our Christmas tree. I wasn't too excited about decorating it that year. It had been a busy week at school, and I was tired. Jonna smiled and asked me not to worry and that she would take care of it, as long as I did the very top for her. As usual, her smile was contagious, and I remember the joy in my heart. You must understand that I am almost five feet, eight inches tall barefooted, but my baby was only five feet, two inches with shoes on. I agreed to this bargain because I could not possibly refuse those big, loving, puppy-dog eyes. I did the top, Jonna did the rest, and it was all finished before Jon got a chance to hang one light.

- Christmas tree—check.
- Christmas Shopping—check.
- Dinner menu—check.
- Cards mailed—check.
- Presents wrapped—check.

The Shackleford family was ready for Christmas Day, and more than eager to celebrate the birthday of our Lord Jesus Christ.

Chapter Nineteen

Fellowship

As CHRISTMAS MORNING DAWNED, so did the sleepy eyes of the Shackleford clan. On our agenda that morning was to first go to celebrate the birth of our Lord Jesus with a Christmas fellowship at church. Afterwards, before going to relatives for family dinner, we opened our gifts. Of course, before we opened ours, the babies of the house got first priority. Yes, we did have little ones, three cats who thought since birth that they must be human . . . There was Casper, brought to our house when Danny and Jonna were little. Next was Cricket, was a "rescued" kitty. She couldn't have been over five months old when she found her way to our front porch. I had gone on an errand, leaving Danny, who was in seventh grade, to babysit. When I got home, there was a little white and black reverse calico kitten sitting on the porch. I was bombarded by "Momma, can we keep her?" I suppose my son Danny was in his seventh-grade wisdom, and pretty much knew I was going to say yes. It's a good thing I loved cats and gave my consent, because unknown to me at that time, both partners in crime had already brought the kitten into the house and fed her. From that moment on, Cricket became a family member. The third one was named Mozart, and was a result of being the only long-haired offspring of Cricket. With a name like Mozart, can't you tell he was my baby? Gift time was good to all three of them. Little stuffed mice, little cat-nip balls, and kitty treats were soon scattered all over the living room floor. Their amusement didn't last, however. They soon turned their attention to the wrapping paper and boxes that had once contained presents for us big kids.

Jon opened some kind of tool that he had mentioned getting. Jonna, of course, unwrapped boxes of various shapes and sizes. But when I opened my gift from her, I found something inside that was unique. I had never received nor owned a gift like this before. My baby had bought a daily journal for me. It was special just because she picked it out for me. But it became more and more special as she told the story of how it came to be in a box that Christmas morning with my name on it.

Jonna said that a friend and she had stood for what seemed like hours trying to find just the right journal for me. She knew that it had to be just the right one because the Lord had put it on her heart to buy a journal. Both girls handled all the journals on the shelf of that store, but still undecided, they asked the Lord which one should be purchased. After that, he directed them to the one he chose, they honored his choice, bought it, and that was that. If you are a momma, you will understand that a gift from a child could have been an old tin can and it would be cherished forever. But that morning, my heart was overflowing. Not only had my little girl thought of me that Christmas, she demonstrated her love for me through it. In fact, no matter how much I loved the diary, the fact that the Lord was in on the decision made this book more special. As we finished unwrapping gifts, Jonna asked me if I would write in it. I promised (which is something I didn't usually do because promises are too easily broken) that on January 1, 2001, I would faithfully write in it for the next 365 days. As you will find out later, I kept my promise. I wrote daily, with the exception of one day that the words just didn't come to me.

Chapter Twenty

The Aside

IN THEATER, OFTEN AN actor will walk to the edge of the stage and talk to the audience. If I am not mistaken, that is called an "aside." At this point, that is what I am attempting to do. I want to add an insert into my story to clarify myself. Until now, the story I have written has come from memories that the Holy Spirit has brought to my recollection. Some have been jotted down on pages of Bibles so I would remember, but the majority has been summoned from my heart by the Lord Jesus through his Holy Spirit. From this point on, there is no need for recollection as the events that I write have been recorded in the precious journal my Jonna bought for me Christmas of 2000. As I promised her that Christmas morning, I have vigilantly recorded each day's events at the close of the day. Nothing written on these pages comes from anything except actual facts as they occurred. As I have said before, this is his book, dedicated *only* for his glory. I know he does nothing without a reason, and the reason for this writing is unknown to me. But as so many things that in my limited wisdom, knowledge, and understanding I can't figure out, I must rely on the Lord Jesus and trust him fully. I want to remind you, my readers, once again to keep an open mind to the power of the Lord and to the infinite wisdom he, as Lord of all, possesses.

Chapter Twenty-One

A Time of Celebration

CHRISTMAS DAY WAS SOON over. I didn't waste much time taking the tree and decorations down, putting them in their boxes, and storing them for another year. What to do now? Jonna and I still had several days of Christmas vacation left before we resumed our daily routine of school and work. Jonna spent most of her days doing "girl stuff" with friends, and I marked off the tasks on a list that I had failed to do before Christmas. As I marked finished accomplishments off of my "to-do" list, I also marked off the days on the calendar as they passed. The next thing I knew, the week had flown by, and it was time to replace 2000 with 2001.

As a tradition, Jonna had spent New Year's Eve night at a friend's house. Jon had stayed up to ring in the new year while I, the old "party pooper," went to bed long before the clock struck 12:00. New Years' Day, 2001, brought the promise of a good new year. In order to have our traditional dinner of ham and beans, as soon as I got out of bed that morning, I pulled out my favorite cooking pot, filled it with ham and beans, seasoned the ingredients, and placed it on the stove to simmer all day. As Jon was still in bed and Jonna still at her friend's, the house was unusually silent. As I was on my way to turn on the television and watch the annual parades, I noticed the journal that was taken out of its box just a few days prior. As I had anxiously waited to start my "daily dairy entries," I decided that I need wait no longer. I retrieved my cup of coffee from the kitchen, found the perfect pen, reclined in my favorite chair, and opened my journal, entitled *Streams in the Desert* by Mrs. Charles E. Cowman.

As I turned to the devotional reading for January 1, this was the Scripture for the day:

> The land whither ye go to possess it is a land of hills and valleys
> and drinketh water of the rain of heaven: a land which the Lord
> thy God careth for; the eyes of the Lord thy God are always upon
> it.

Deuteronomy 11:11–12 (KJV)

I remember thinking, What a perfect Scripture for the first day of the New Year. Just as Moses was leading the Israelites to a new land which was unknown to them, I was being led into a new year. Within the 365 days this year was to bring, I had no clue what would come my way. At that moment, the Holy Spirit brought to my remembrance "Keep your eyes on me. Do not turn to the left or the right." In no way had I forgotten these words before that moment, but it was just one of those times I guess the Lord thought he needed to remind me. Anyway, as I read the rest of the devotional for January 1, 2001, I searched for the highlighter that was lying on the table next to me and highlighted these words:

> We cannot tell what loss and sorrow and trial are doing. Trust
> only. The Father comes near to take our hand and lead us on our
> way today. It shall be a good, a blessed new year!

As I have said, my limited wisdom is nothing compared to the wisdom of God. In other words, I never completely grasped the entire meaning of this passage . . . not until now. (Remember this journal was written twenty years ago and has not been opened nor read until this day, February 24, 2021.)

My spirit being filled by the devotional, I took my trusted pen in hand and wrote the following entry for January 1, 2001:

> This is an awesome day in the Lord. My rest and comfort lie
> only in you, my Father. I ask you to always use me however you
> need me and to make me your messenger so others will feel you
> through me. I have so much to be thankful for.

By that time, Jon was up scrounging around in the kitchen, and the kitties were running through the house playing. I thought I was finished with my first journal entry of the New Year, but I was wrong. The Lord put on my heart to write something to Jonna in it. Then in the future, I would give it back to her containing the thoughts and emotions of her momma.

I turned to a blank page in the journal and wrote these words:

This is for my Jonna and for whomever she wants to share it with someday when I am too old or unable to comfort you. Probably in a year's time, I will have felt lots of things that you will feel. Even though you may not understand why I wrote what I did, the feeling I had will come to you by my love and God's Spirit. I'll always love you, my precious angel! God loved me so I would know how to love you so you'll know how to love your family, on and on. Always remember that our Lord is the source of our being and he will always be your true friend when everyone else will let you down from time to time. Listen to the Lord, my love, and your life will be blessed many, many times over. I love you forever and always.

—Momma

With this added notation, I closed the book and finished my coffee.

Chapter Twenty-Two

Prophecy

FOR THE NEXT PART of my story, I will be writing from the journal during the year 2001. I will include prophecies that were given to Jonna and myself. As I realize this book is Jonna's story, I think you will find that in order for God's glory to completely shine through this writing, prophecies told to me must be included.

Do you recall the prophecy that was given to me in the fall of 2000? Just in case you don't, please let me remind you that the Lord's message to me was "You will face a great tribulation. Do not turn to the left or the right, but keep your eyes on me." Yes, that's the one. As time passed, the Holy Spirit brought these words to my remembrance frequently. This is weird! Early on in January, on my way to church, the voice of God came to me and told me that "My task is at hand. Do not be afraid because I am with you." I asked him if I'd know what the task was and that I wasn't afraid because I knew he was preparing me for it.

"Do not look to the left or the right," the Lord responded. "Keep my eyes upon him. My Spirit is within you and my Spirit will speak through you."

Yes, for those of you wondering what I meant by the "voice" of God, I recognize the voice of my Lord.

Jesus says in John 10:26, "My sheep hear my voice, and I know them, and they follow me."

I remember all the times that these words came to me while driving, reading, cooking, cleaning, or whatever I was doing. The Holy Spirit would randomly choose any time that I was silent and willing to listen. For that, I always gave him thanks

Many, many times after hearing him speak to me, I would think that whatever he was preparing me for *must* be something really important. In a nutshell, whatever my tribulation or upcoming task was, my precious Lord Jesus was going out of his way to make sure that I wasn't afraid. Now, I ask you, Who else but Jesus would love me that much to take care of me over an event that hasn't even happened yet?

During these times, I was often led to read the following Scripture:

> Have I not commanded thee? Be strong and of a good courage;
> be not afraid, neither be thou dismayed; for the Lord thy God is
> with thee whithersoever thou goest.

Joshua 1:9.

As a result, this verse is forever ingrained in my mind. Many would call it my Life Verse, but I just know it's the verse of Scripture that I now live by. I am not afraid of much. I am hesitant and cautious at times, but certainly not fearful. As you continue to read, I am convinced you will understand why Joshua 1:9 is the Scripture I now live by.

I knew in my heart that no matter what road the Lord was preparing me for that I would be ready for it. I realized that there was no road I would travel that Jesus didn't walk down. In fact, there was nothing that I would experience that Jesus didn't ordain to happen. If that be the case, then there was nothing that I should fear, right?

Jesus paved this road long before my feet would leave their footprints on it. No matter how bumpy the road would get, I knew Jesus was at the finish line waiting for me. It was this knowledge that the Holy Spirit would remind me of. It was my Jesus that would hold my hand, and it will be my Lord who will wait for me at the end of the passage. Tribulation or not, I AM okay.

Not long after, Jonna started experiencing minor trials. What seemed trivial to me was earth shattering to my baby. Ups and downs with her friends, daily hassles at work, and studies were part of her life. She took each day in stride, but she was having trouble letting go at the end of the day. Often during our nightly talks, she would let go of built-up emotions through tears. I would hold her, let her cry, and tell her that tomorrow will be better. I knew she wasn't happy, but I firmly believed the life of any eighteen-year-old girl could be emotionally hard. At least I comforted myself with these words, but I knew within my heart that Jonna was hurting deeply, far more than I realized. I just couldn't pinpoint the true reason for her pain. Call it a mother's intuition, spiritual discernment, or both. All I knew was that something was going on within my little girl's spirit.

Finally, one night while I was reading, I overheard Jonna talking to a friend over the phone. Her voice was trembling as she conveyed whatever was troubling her. The conversation lasted a good while, but I couldn't make out Jonna's words through the tears. "Enough is enough," I stated to myself, or maybe out loud to whomever might have heard. After my feet pushed down the reclining leg of my rocking chair, I stood up and went straight for Jonna's bedroom. I was going to find out what was wrong regardless of the confrontation that might be awaiting. To my surprise, my weepy-eyed daughter looked up at me, started crying harder that she had previously been, and proceeded to inform me on the details of her crisis. These words summed it up: "Momma, nobody likes me."

Now, please consider all the characteristics and strengths Jonna has had since birth. Given all of the essentials for a person full of self-confidence, would you not believe this daring young woman to be full of an "I can do anything through Christ who strengthens me" attitude toward herself? When a task came from the Lord, she was full of fight and ready to battle whomever or whatever might have stood in her way. However, at that moment, I was looking upon one of the most humble children of the Lord that you could imagine.

I softly tried to relay the message that everybody liked her. "Jonna," I said, "I have watched you every school day for four years. I see how others react to you. I notice regularly how people love to be around you. Especially the little ones. The grade-school kids all know you by name. They just wait for you to show them attention because it makes them feel so special. Your friends love you. I know some of the kids don't care for you, but do you know why? It's because they are intimidated by you. They can't compare themselves to a beautiful, intelligent, successful, and loving you. That's their problem, not yours. One day, they will realize the heartache they have caused you and hopefully regret their decision. Why in the world would you think that nobody liked you?"

With that question being asked, Jonna smiled a quirky little grin, told me she loved me, and left it at that. Did I ever find out why she felt this way? Somewhat, but I don't believe I ever knew the whole story.

For several years, Jonna had talked about going on to college to major in psychology. She had an avid compassion for children and had involvement with little ones harboring deep depression over hurtful issues, and she knew she wanted to help those in distress. Jonna loved the Words of Jesus in Matthew 19:14, which said:

> But Jesus said, "Suffer little children, and forbid them not, to come unto me; for of such is the kingdom of heaven."

To say she had compassion for these little ones was truly an understatement. She carried the wounds of any child just as a mother would. Because of this and because she felt that this was the direction the Lord wanted her to go, that was her mission in life. She had decided she was going to "touch the lives of thousands" by ministering to the little children.

I use the term "touch the lives of thousands" literally because these words were spoken to her by prophecy. One particular Sunday morning back in late fall, she announced that she was going to church with us. We had prayed together for the Lord to release her from this bondage, and when she received her schedule for the next week her boss had given her Sunday off. So that Sunday morning, the three of us piled in the car and headed for our little church building down the highway.

During church, the Holy Spirit kept urging me to take Jonna to the altar. Our church was solely led by the Holy Spirit; therefore, the altar was open to anyone at any time during the service. It was toward the end of the message that I couldn't stand it any longer. I reached over, took Jonna's hand, and down the aisle we went to the altar.

The pastor continued preaching while we prayed. Almost immediately, the assistant pastor stooped down in front of us. She relayed a message that the Lord had given her to tell Jonna. I will never forget her words and the tears flowing down my baby's face as she heard the prophecy which simply said, "You will touch the lives of thousands." I squeezed her hand, she squeezed it back, and leaned toward me for a hug. I put my arms around her and held her while she sobbed. In just a few moments, she broke the hold and stepped away. Amidst the flow of tears was a smile, one that I interpreted with no difficulty at all. The grin on her face was peaceful, serene, and one of joy. I was so relieved that she was mentally at rest.

Later that day, she stated to me that she now was for certain that the Lord wanted her to counsel children.

"Momma, I am gonna touch the lives of thousands of little ones that need help," she revealed confidently. Once again, I pondered this in my heart with joy.

The certainty of her future had begun to disappear during the winter. At different times, I would overhear her tell others that she wasn't sure what she wanted to do after college nor what the Lord wanted her to do, either.

Yes, mommas sometimes eavesdrop.

I didn't approach her with the words I heard. I knew my baby, and I was well aware she would mention it to me one day or another. Well, that day never did come. She never discussed it with me, and in time, I just decided that maybe I overheard incorrectly. I figured that I was making a mountain out of a molehill. After all, I felt that I shouldn't have been listening in the first place.

Chapter Twenty-Three

Minister

THE WINTER MONTH OF January passed by quickly. Nothing unusual had happened at school for either Jonna or me. Jonna was still working after school. The "pressing" issues of her life were once again on the forefront. Jonna found herself trying to minister to friends, witness to unsaved friends and enemies, and not be broken down by those who rejected her Christianity. She followed the Lord's lead in her daily activities.

"Momma, I have two responsibilities on earth," she declared, "school and work. I just figure that I can fit Jesus into both of them and do his work."

She did that very thing. She would never fail to give Jesus praise and honor wherever she went.

February arrived. Valentine's Day at Crab Orchard School always brought anticipation because on that day flowers were delivered to students. The flowers were ordered two or three weeks in advance by anyone choosing to send a Valentine's Day flower to someone special. Teachers could send a carnation to faculty, staff, or students. Students could send the symbols of love to teachers, staff, or other students. In fact, many parents ordered a flower for their own children or a teacher. Overall, it was just a lot of fun. I would stand at the door of my classroom at the end of the day just to see how many flowers individual students had received. Some carried home several, others packed just a few, but almost everyone received at least one. It's amazing how happy people become when they realize that someone cares about them. The joyful laughter throughout the school on Valentine's Day was awesome to hear. But it was that particular Valentines' Day that I had begun to notice that Jonna's laughter wasn't as loud as it had always been.

Jonna had ordered a carnation for several of her friends and teachers that year. Momma got one, too. She was so excited over Valentine's Day. But as soon as school was over, she stopped by my classroom before leaving for work. She had only two flowers, one from a girlfriend and one from Momma. The flower she had anticipated for days didn't come. The *one* flower that was in her hopes and dreams didn't show up. Because of this, Jonna felt dejected and lost. I remember the sadness of her beautiful face when she shared the realization that "maybe" that someone special didn't feel the same way she did.

Once again, I didn't know how to help her. I knew all too well that relationships usually come and go, but what could I possibly say that would make her feel better at that given moment. I just told her how much I understood and that some men just don't get as excited about Valentine's Day as women. It seemed like a pretty lame thing to say to my hurting baby, but that's what came out. After a few minutes, she informed me that she felt better and had to go to work. We exchanged I love yous and left it at that.

February's days were passing quickly. It seemed as though I didn't see Jonna much during that month. Her work schedule was juggled back and forth around school and extracurricular stuff. Among the grind of her daily schedule, ACT and SAT tests were rapidly approaching. Being the perfectionist she was, studying for them was a must. The tests were conducted on Saturdays, which only meant less time she was at home. This mom understood all too well that the life of an eighteen-year-old was a start to their independence. I didn't honestly like the idea that my youngest child was all grown up. I just didn't like it one bit. I remembered the day that my son left for college in Laramie, Wyoming. I cried for days. What in the world was I going to do when my baby left home? Thank goodness she was going to one of the junior colleges in southern Illinois because that would allow me a couple of more years before having to cut the apron strings completely. (I don't think it's possible for this momma to ever cut her apron strings completely. Just ask Danny!) Anyway, the fact was, my Jonna wasn't a little girl anymore.

By the end of February, students of Crab Orchard High School were discussing prom. Now when I was in high school, many moons ago, the girls sat back and hoped that the "man of their dreams" would ask them to prom. In fact, some of us just hoped that "anyone" would ask them to prom. It was unheard of for the female gender to invite a male.

Boy, how things change!

In the year 2001, it was socially correct for anyone to ask anyone of the opposite sex. Jonna took a giant step. I say "giant" because I tried to instill in my children that men should be men and women should be women and not interfere in the role of a man. I am probably getting some snide remarks at this point from readers, but I do believe that men should do the inviting, open car doors, and take care of things. But that's beside the point in my story, thank goodness! Jonna stepped up and invited that someone special. However, she hadn't yet received an answer. At least not yet.

Chapter Twenty-Four

Gifted

As THE WINTRY MONTH of February came to an end, the month of March made its first appearance, roaring like a lion. Even though winter had decided to stay around for a while, the Crab Orchard girls started playing softball in order for the coach to determine the players for the 2001 team. Amid the uncertainty of who her escort would be for her senior prom, I could always count on seeing the radiance in her face when softball practice was over. Practices were going well, even better than I expected for my young athlete.

"Momma!" She ran into the house one evening after practice. "You will never guess what happened at practice! Coach asked me for my opinion on the girls trying out. Momma, am I really that good that he would consider how I feel about the team?"

The answer to her question was a no-brainer! Without any hesitation or consideration of the right words to say, I responded, "Yes, Baby Girl! You are that good."

I have mentioned before that Jonna loved to win, but who doesn't? This isn't the kind of competitive nature that I instilled in my daughter. She had no problem with being a sore loser. The problem came when she felt as if she had not competed to her personal best. The dreadful competition which she could not tolerate losing was against herself. That evening, any doubts about her ability to excel in the sport of softball were squelched. In her opinion, she had finally reached a level of self-acceptance that she had strived for. Jonna never lacked in self-confidence when it came to a task she was determined to complete. She knew that she was musically inclined, academically gifted, and artistically talented.

She had no problems with any task dealing with these areas. What she lacked so desperately was self-esteem—namely down on her outward appearance. All through high school, we discussed and greatly disagreed on her outward beauty. Many times I held her in my arms while tears rolled down her olive-skinned face because she thought there was no beauty to be found in her.

Time after time I tried to convince her that she was beautiful on the outside, but more importantly was the beauty she possessed deep within her spirit. Even though she had indeed inherited the "best" of her parent's outward genetics, the traits of her spirit were incomprehensibly beautiful.

The fruits of the Spirit poured out of her.

For those who don't know what I am talking about, the fruits of the Spirit are the characteristics of the Holy Spirit. If you are a child of God, these fruits should be manifested continually in your lifestyle. These characteristics of the Spirit of God are how others recognize God's children. In Galatians 5:22, the Apostle Paul lists them:

> But the fruit of the Spirit is love, joy, peace, longsuffering, gentleness, goodness, faith, meekness, temperance:

Many times I have heard others say that she looked like her daddy on the outside, but she had her momma's heart. Well, I will be the first one to admit that these words are a wonderful compliment to me, but no matter how much I wanted to, I could not take credit for the radiant spirit of my baby. The truth, the whole truth, and nothin' but the truth was this—it had nothing to do with her mother.

Please, let me explain. Jonna was always a sweet little girl, but still yet, a little girl with all the ups and downs of typical childhood. She definitely recalled the lessons that had life taught her, but it wasn't until she surrendered that precious heart to her Lord Jesus at age eleven that I began to see her inward spirit becoming transformed into the spirit of a young woman whose path was ordained by the Lord, well before she was even a thought in my mind. You see, too many of us make a decision to accept the salvation of our Lord Jesus, but don't make a conscious decision to live by his commandments, walk in obedience to him, or to allow his Spirit to dictate our life. We have what Scripture calls a "shallow" faith.

Jonna's faith was never "shallow" nor unseen. She lived to the ultimate calling of the Lord. She gave herself completely to Jesus and his will. She lived daily by the motto "What would Jesus do?"

Because of her dedication to his service, the Holy Spirit within her was continually allowed to grow. Let me clarify that the Holy Spirit didn't grow within her, but the portion of the Holy Spirit's presence grew. In other words, the fruit of the Holy Spirit grew stronger and stronger within my little girl. The result? Jonna's daily admirable and beautiful spirit reflected the light of the Spirit of God. She knew this and desired this, but still because of the humbleness Jonna contained, her beauty of any kind was never within her comprehension. From the time that my bundle of joy was about eleven years old, I often heard the words, "Momma, why am I not as pretty as this person?" or "Momma, nobody likes me. I am too fat and ugly."

I understood the true meaning of her words. I understood the message that echoed from the air waves was literal and heartfelt. Year after year, my ears would receive the audible message my little girl sent to me. Time after time, I understood the battle of outward appeal versus inward beauty that was a constant demon within Jonna's heart. Every time I felt the spiritual warfare of what truly constituted the definition of beauty penetrating from her spirit (Yes, I could "see" into my daughter's spirit. Aren't all mommas supposed to be that aware of their children's feelings?), I always prayed that one day she would be able to see herself as others saw her. My prayer was most definitely answered, but not in my definition of time. Many times in my walk with the Lord Jesus, the Holy Spirit has brought to my remembrance the Scripture that the Apostle Peter penned around the year 66 AD:

> But, beloved, be not ignorant of this one thing, that one day is with the Lord as a thousand years, and a thousand years as one day.

2 Peter 3:8

I have learned that the timetable for life that had been carved into the souls of human nature since the industrial age invented the clock has NO existence within the scheme of the heavens. Our Father does not dictate his perfect will according to time as we understand it. Jehovah created time. His time is eternal and never ending. Therefore, did my prayer for Jonna to realize how beautiful she was go unanswered? Not a chance! My prayer was just not yet to be realized. However, the day that I could honestly know that my beautiful angel understood the true meaning of beauty was drawing nearer.

Chapter Twenty-Five:

Dwindling of the Spirit

By the thirteenth day of March, Jonna's date for her senior prom was determined. To this day, I am not sure which of them did the asking or if it was a mutual decision, but she was to attend prom with a young man whom she had dated early on in high school. Way too many times when a relationship is over, friendship isn't an option. This relationship never faded, however. The two kept a friendship status and talked often. Even though it was for only prom night, the two would once again be a "couple." Jonna was overjoyed with this arrangement. After all, the two made a very attractive pair. Through the excitement, however, I could sense that there were deeper emotions being stirred within my Jonna.

I knew that she had something on her mind, something that was overshadowing her daily life. Yet, once again, she had shown no signs of a willingness to discuss any thoughts with me. I decided to still give her time. I never had to pry into Jonna's business. We shared lots of things in our nightly discussions. As a result, I felt confident that she told me whatever I needed to know. I had confidence that if she didn't bring it up, I didn't need to hear it. But even at that, we usually talked about it anyway. I had great faith in the maturity and logic of my daughter's decision to follow the Lord's guidance. I knew she was following his lead and in him I had complete trust.

Jonna's issues were finally at rest for a little while. Everything was proceeding smoothly in her life. Softball, work, school, social life, and spiritual life were all in check.

On March 13, 2001, I realized that my spiritual life was dwindling. I suppose I had been taking for granted the prophecy given to me last Thanksgiving. I suppose that my spiritual high had peaked. I supposed that maybe the prophecy wasn't going to be anything major after all. I do believe that my suppositions were wrong! Well, it's not funny how the Lord sometimes allows us to think we are doing everything we should be for him and then show us that the ground we are standing on isn't as solid as we assume.

Feeling very secure in my spiritual life at that time, I had a spiritual "alert" while cooking dinner that particular night. While I was setting the supper table, Jonna walked into the kitchen. She would often stroll into the kitchen to see what was on the stove or to sneak a bite while she stirred the contents of a pot. However, this time, she was just standing there staring at me. Even though there wasn't a word spoken, I could feel that there was something important she needed to say.

Telepathy or a spiritual connection? I prefer the latter, but it didn't matter either way.

The still, small voice within me was telling me to put the dishes down and listen to my baby girl. As soon as I set the dinner plates on the table and looked at Jonna, she revealed the words that had been building within her for several weeks. As I looked closer, I noticed the tears that were welled up in her eyes and without any ado, I asked what was wrong with no hesitation. I will never, ever, or forever more forget the message that my daughter gave me that night. With watery eyes, but a smiling face, she answered, "Momma, don't take this the wrong way 'cause I love you with all my heart. But I don't fit here. I want to go home."

I heard the message loud and clear, but didn't listen! I remember telling her that God's children were just passing through this life and that if we were a true child of God, we would feel that way. We talked a few more minutes before she went back into her room to finish homework. Double wow, you could say. While I finished dinner that night, Jesus and I had a *big* talk. Now, I definitely knew that something was bothering my little girl. I knew beyond a shadow of a doubt that she had a major burden. But what was it?

As I talked to Jesus about the worry I felt for her and the heartache I was experiencing because she was hurting, I heard the voice of my Lord once again remind me, "Your task is at hand. Don't turn to the right or the left, but keep your eyes on me." Before I could get the words "I am" from my mouth, the Lord added, "Regain your focus. Focus on my face."

With the completion of his message, I realized that I had been dwindling in my spiritual walk, not in a major way, but just enough to let my guard down with the subtle darts that Satan was going to eventually throw at me. I realized that in no way, shape, or form, could I lose any spiritual strength or crack any window for which Satan could sneak in. With that being said, my faith, trust, and strength in the Lord Jesus once again continued to grow, and the growth continued on to take me to a spiritual closeness with my Jesus that I only dreamed about in the past.

Daily, I praised and thanked him for what he was allowing to take place in my spirit, because I never imagined being so close to someone who loved me so very much.

The anxiety I felt over Jonna's words that night seemed to fade in a couple of days. I believed that I stopped worrying so much because I had decided that she was just down in the dumps over something or someone. This deep compassion could be infiltrating her heart because she was carrying a burden for someone else or because she was disappointed over something that she didn't share with me. Either way, in complete trust, I asked Jesus to help her with whatever it was. In complete trust, I asked him to hold Jonna in his arms. Yet while trusting completely in him, the words she said were placed in my heart!

Chapter Twenty-Six

Jubilation

THE MONTH OF MARCH progressed rapidly. For me, March was always a month where, as my grandma used to say, "I don't know my head from a hole in the ground."

The cold winds of the month always ushered in Illinois state vocal contests. At least three Saturdays of the month were spent with soloists, ensembles, and choirs from school. The hectic six-day work weeks made time drift off the calendar faster than I could imagine. Jonna's softball schedule was full-blown, and the hours she worked after school and weekends were rapidly producing signs of fatigue in my baby. However, in the midst of blustery days, schedules, and stress, unexpected blessings are always welcomed. I received a visit from Jonna's coach during class one day. He had traveled down the hallway of the old yet wonderful high school building to give me news that I didn't expect. Even though the news was unexpected, the message did not surprise me.

Coach had just received a call from a softball scout who was recruiting for a college softball team for the next school year. He had heard of Jonna from various other coaches who had seen her play and wanted to come to a game, watch her, and talk to her. Of course, this momma agreed without hesitation, and gave the okay to set it up with the scout. Because I knew exactly which classroom my young budding athlete was sitting in at that moment, I asked the teacher next door if she would monitor my classroom for a few minutes.

After she told me yes, I headed upstairs to the English room, asked the teacher if I could talk to Jonna, and waited patiently outside of the classroom door until she appeared in the hallway.

I will never forget the concerned expression on her face as she asked me if something was wrong. She knew that I wouldn't have left my class unless it concerned something of importance. As well as I remember her worrisome expression, I can just as easily recall the jubilation on her face that soon replaced the concern.

As I relayed the news of a college scout's interest, tears started welling up in her chocolate-brown eyes. She didn't say anything; she stood in the hallway and cried.

"Why the tears?" I asked.

"Happy tears, Momma!" she replied.

As I finished telling her that the coach was setting it all up, she regained her composure and hugged me.

"I'm okay now. See ya at noon, Momma!" Jonna said.

As I walked back to my classroom to review the "damage" my unattended junior high choir had done, I prayed, "Lord Jesus, this is such an honor for my baby. I just ask you to watch over her, lead and guide her to make sure that she walks according to your will."

If you are a momma, you will understand that even though I *knew* that the Holy Spirit was alive within her and that Jesus was paving the path he wanted her to travel, I still had to pray for my baby.

It was just a few days later, at the next home game, that I walked out of my classroom toward the softball field to watch the game. I didn't see anything unusual. Jonna's dad was sitting on the bench in our designated spot and the players were out in the field warming up. Just as I was getting closer to the field, however, I noticed the team's coach talking to an unrecognized face. I entertained the notion that maybe it was the college scout, and as a result, I hurried toward Jonna's dad to see if I was correct.

To my delight, Jon had already been introduced to him and said that I would get to meet him later. In no time at all, I saw that the two men had left the dugout and were coming toward us. Introductions were made, the coach went back to the dugout full of girls, and the scout sat down on the bench next to Jon. I tried to hear every word that was exchanged between Jon and the scout, but most of the conversation was about the game, about plays, about various umpire calls, etc.

I soon became bored trying to eavesdrop when it didn't concern the star catcher, so I just decided to watch the game. I figured being a cheerleader from the stand was more important at that moment. However, this momma's ears were never completely tuned out from the men's conversation. I overheard enough of the talking to know it was okay to go back to the plays of the softball game.

After the game was over, the softball recruiter stood up from the wooden bench and began a conversation with Jonna's dad that I overheard. Needless to say, he was greatly impressed with her catching and batting abilities, but they were not the predominant talent that he detected. He had noticed a characteristic Jonna possessed that he hadn't expected. He was fascinated by her ability to manage the game from the catcher's stance behind home plate, but he was more interested in the way she was able to "keep the team together." He commented on the admiration the other players gave her and the compassion that she showed the other players. I believe the words "She was the glue that held the team together" danced in my ears when they were spoken.

I realized at that moment that this college scout had to be a Christian man because he recognized her talent, but he saw into her spirit. He thanked Jon and me for allowing him the courtesy of joining us for the game, and with that being said, he walked to the dugout to meet my baby.

I was still a bit nervous as I waited for their meeting to be finished, so I decided to walk back into the school building and get something to drink out the Coke machine. Sure enough, as I was walking back to the softball field with a Diet Coke in my hand, I noticed the scout leaving the dugout and Jonna picking up her equipment. I couldn't help but notice the happiness that she was sending my way as she looked up the little hill toward me. The closer her steps took her, the bigger her smile looked. Upon approaching the parking lot, however, her first words were not about the game, the scout, or their discussion. As soon as she had put her catching gear in the car, she looked at me and said, "Momma, I'm starving. Got anything to eat?" Yep! That's my Jonna . . .

I went back into school and visited the vending machine. Chips and a package of M&M's were retrieved from the drop slot in the machine.

"He wants me to come to the college and talk after school tomorrow, so I will have to call work and explain that I can't be there," Jonna said as I gave them to her.

I could tell from the tone in her voice that she was elated, but I had to ask if she really wanted this.

"I will tell you after I talk to him tomorrow," she told me.

Chapter Twenty-Seven

Serenity and Peace

IT WAS HARD TO get to sleep that night. I couldn't help but think about what Lord Jesus wanted Jonna to do. It seemed that every time my mind relaxed enough to drift off in sleep, I would be awakened by Satan's blast of doubt. I was so excited for my baby girl. I was so proud of her accomplishments academically, so happy for her sports achievements, and so at ease with the choices she had made so far.

But the greatest blessing I, as a mother, could have received was the spiritual decisions she had made since she became a child of the King six years ago. This particular night, however, my spirit was restless over the decision she would make tomorrow regarding a college scholarship based on softball skills. If you will remember, Jonna had received dozens of invitations to visit various colleges throughout the United States based on her academic achievements and ACT scores. I was much keener on the idea that she would attend a more academically-inclined institution. She and I talked often about one particular college located in the Shenandoah Valley. I myself would have chosen that one for her. However, this wasn't my choice to make. My beautiful, intelligent, well-rounded baby wasn't a baby any longer. She was an eighteen-year-old young woman, and even though she still asked for my advice on decisions that needed to be made, she didn't always take my advice.

Mom was her second advisor. Jesus was her primary counsel. I was very secure with that, too, because he certainly was much more intelligent than I. In fact, he could see further down the road paved for his daughter and knew his will for her present and future steps. Even with that serene peace I so well knew, I realized sleep wasn't much of an option and decided to slip out of bed.

As I walked down the hallway to the living room, I wasn't at all surprised to see Jonna's bedroom light on. Many nights, I would wake up
to see a dim light seeping through the darkness of the hallway. I always
knew that my little night owl was doing one of two things. Once in a
while she would be talking on the phone with her best friend, brother,
or sister-in-law. However, the majority of her sleepless nights were filled
with Bible reading and prayer. On this night, enveloped with indecision
and anticipation, I opened her cracked bedroom door to find her talking
things over with Jesus. She looked up as the sound of the door brushing
over the carpet alerted her that someone was there.

I immediately saw a glow around my child—a brilliance that could
only signify one thing. Jonna was deep into the realm of the Holy Spirit's
presence. With just a small knowledge of the spiritual world we are allowed to travel to with the Holy Spirit's aid, I knew enough to recognize
the sign that I should just walk away, go into the living room as I had
planned, and let the Holy Spirit do his bidding with my baby. As I turned
around to do just this, I overheard my angel girl continue in prayer as if
nothing had disturbed her "spiritual encounter of the God kind" (as my
husband calls it).

My heart rejoiced. The words of the Lord Jesus pounded upon my
brain, saying:

> Consider the lilies of the field, how they grow; they toil not, nei-
> ther do they spin: and yet I say unto you, that even Solomon in
> all his glory was not arrayed like one of these. Wherefore, if God
> so clothe the grass of the field, which today is, and tomorrow is
> cast into the oven, shall he not much more clothe you, O ye of
> little faith?

Matthew 6:28–30

That was my scolding for doubting that the Lord Jesus would direct
Jonna's decision tomorrow. My precious Lord Jesus does, indeed, scold us
from time to time. The words that stood out in this Scripture were "O ye
of little faith." I suppose that even Christian mommas who *know* that the
Lord God will take care of her children, we let our guard down and try
to carry the burden. Yet, when the Holy Spirit brought the words "O ye
of little faith" to my remembrance, a sudden flow of heavenly, God-given
peace penetrated throughout my entire being. As quickly as the words

came to me, I could feel myself release the worry concerning my baby's decision.

I remember speaking these words as I quietly returned to bed: "Okay, Lord Jesus! I got the message! Thank you for giving me peace, and thank you for guiding my baby girl. I love you so much!"

Having said my quick prayer of gratitude, I climbed back into bed, listened to my husband snore, noticed my kitty snoozing way on my pillow, pulled the covers up around me, and drifted away in peaceful slumber.

Needless to say, the alarm went off way too early that morning. As part of our usual routine, I hesitantly climbed out of bed and strolled to the kitchen to make coffee and breakfast. On a daily basis, when breakfast was made, I would wake up Jonna. She would eat while I got ready for school. I would wash breakfast dishes, etc., while she was readying herself for her day. As a rule, she was in her truck and pulling out of the driveway long before I was finished preparing to go.

As I was making the bed that morning, I heard my quiet little angel bellow, "Momma, come here. I need to tell you something."

Most mornings we were in such a rush to get chores completed that we didn't take the time to have a detailed discussion about anything. However, because of the seriousness in her voice this morning, I felt the need to overlook any unessentional task so that a mother/daughter conversation could be held.

"Momma, you know me and Jesus talked last night," she began. "He told me that I would know what he wanted me to do. He said that after I talked to the softball scout today, I would have no doubt what to do."

I asked her if she had any idea at this point, and she said, "Nope. Not in the least. But I will before long."

If I were an artist, and I could paint emotions, I would paint the confidence and surety of Jonna's faith in the Lord's words she had heard the night before. Let's see, what colors in God's mighty spectrum would possibly reflect the secure and doubtless faith my baby possessed? Perhaps purple? After all, that is the color of royalty. Maybe blue? No, blue is too calming. Red! Of course, red! Red shows strength and boldness. The brilliance of the color red was the color on God's palette that defined the faith my baby stood for. The confidence she had in her Lord and his spoken word was absolutely astonishing. Jonna didn't take the word of God lightly. She meditated on revelations of the word daily with an understanding that could only be given by the great and mighty teacher, the Holy Spirit.

"The Bible means what it means! Just read it and see!" she would often say.

Jonna's decisiveness concerning the Father, Jesus, and the Holy Spirit was unshakeable. The words of a song that was often sung at our church come to mind. "I shall not be, I shall not be moved. Just like a tree standing by the water, I shall not be moved." So it was with the faith of my daughter. She could not be moved in her walk with the Lord.

Chapter Twenty-Eight

Soulmates

AFTER OUR CONVERSATION THAT morning, we parted ways as she headed toward the highway directed for Marion High School for her early-morning class, and I instinctively took a routine turn down a country lane which for seven years had become my shortcut to Crab Orchard, Illinois.

I engaged in my morning schedule with approximately 95 percent focus. If my classes hadn't been filled with the eagerness of children from the kindergarten through third grade classes and the challenges of keeping a junior high choir on task, whatever academic and musical focus I possessed would have been greatly reduced that morning. When the bell rang for lunch, I hurried to the cafeteria to find out how my baby's morning had transpired.

As I walked through the door of the lunchroom, I looked over to the chairs and rectangular lunch table where Jonna and her circle of Christian friends, who had known each other since the first year of high school, would sit. These were the friends that the Lord sent to Jonna. These were definitely not the only friends that my daughter had made in her high school cafeteria, where my "kids" assembled daily to share the morning's activities while sharing lunches. I always felt a reassuring peace the moment I saw them, and they were her Christian "soulmates," the kind of friends that stay with you for a lifetime and beyond.

There are so many events that are eternally etched into the portals of my memory concerning this precious circle of friends. I will forever be able to call such memories up from the depths of moments recorded into the files of the life of Christy Shackleford.

While my fingers type the words the Holy Spirit dictates, I am recollecting a few of those blessed memories. No, I am not exaggerating about multitasking abilities. During my high school years, I bombarded myself with every business class afforded to me. Accounting I, Accounting II, Typing I, Typing II, Stenography I, Stenography II (or should I say the old-fashioned kind of dictation that involves crooked lines and patterns for each phonetic sound of the English language) were my forte. Therefore, my ability to type while I listen and still have a roving mind is very believable.

I know the previous paragraph has nothing really to do with my story; however, I want my readers to feel at ease with the words that are written in this story. I don't want to incur any doubt among those who are diligently trying to understand that any word written on these pages is truthful and not exaggerated.

With that being said, let's go back to Jonna and her friends. Through the last couple of years, I have unknowingly walked in a room finding two or more, sometimes a small bunch, of these wonderfully awesome children of God praying for an answer, guidance, a need, a healing, or simply offering up praise to the King of Kings. I have watched as they prayed together in the anointing of the Spirit while laying hands upon whoever needed a "touch of the Spirit." I have many times sat either behind or in front of some of them while attending a church service and heard the most beautiful "tongues of angels" escape from the mouths of these young men and women of God. Talk about a blessing!

For any mature child of God to be able to hear and see the Holy Spirit's anointing and baptism on his younger saints is a spectacular blessing. Talk about a bigger blessing? To hear and see the Holy Spirit's baptism and power within your own child is . . . priceless. I often refer to lyrics of songs because it seems the Holy Spirit often brings the words of songs to my remembrance. He does this to make sure I hear his meanings. What else would a music major relate to more clearly? Of course, the most defined way that I hear his meaning is when he directly speaks to me. Right now, as I speak of the blessed memories that I hold, I hear the words, "precious memories, how they linger"—ringing in my ears.

As my writings of that particular day in my daughter's life continue, after feeling the daily inner calm upon seeing the daily lunchtime routine, I walked to the lunch table hoping to hear that the Lord had already given Jonna some kind of guidance toward the college that had expressed interest in her attendance there. Upon feeling my presence behind her back, she intuitively turned toward me, smiled, and said, "Not yet, Momma."

As I have stated before, Jonna and I had a spiritual connection. In other words, she knew me pretty darn well. As this was the answer that I had anticipated, but not really wanted, I leaned over, kissed the top of her chocolate-brown hair, and directed myself to the salad bar to decide what I wanted to eat. As my thoughts were then centered upon an amazing choice of salad entrées, I couldn't help but hear giggling from the lunch table. Needless to say, my heart was overjoyed. If I haven't mentioned it before, I will say now that among the many "precious memories" I have are the ones that Jonna and I shared daily during her four years of high school.

My afternoon classes were not completed before Jonna's scheduled appointment with the softball scout. Jonna's class schedule was fulfilled for the day at about 1:35, and as a result she was allowed to leave the school campus for the day. Before heading for the parking lot to unlock her truck, she stuck her head through my classroom door.

"Bye, Momma! I'm leaving. See ya when I get home."

I will never forget the response from my high school choir members who were supposed to be rehearsing for the upcoming spring concert. "Where's she going?" several of them remarked. As I told them the story, I was very careful to make sure that they understood that this decision was being made by the Lord. I know that teachers aren't allowed to talk about Jesus within a classroom environment anymore. Well, guess what? We weren't supposed to twenty years ago, either. But of the students seated in my classroom at that moment, 99 percent of them had been my students since they were in grade school, and they already knew my relationship with the Lord Jesus.

Besides, I didn't care one way or another. As my daughter continued to display boldness in the name of the Lord Jesus, so did I. As my spiritual strength didn't start its walk to maturity much sooner that Jonna was given the gifts of the Spirit, I'm not sure which of us the greater influence was. Either way, aren't children of God supposed to stand for Jesus? Jesus told his disciples:

> Whosoever therefore shall confess me before men, him will I confess also before my Father which is in heaven. But whosoever shall deny me before men, him will I also deny before my Father which is in heaven.

Matthew 10: 32–33

Driving home from school was about a thirty-five-minute trip, and it was during that time that I would conduct a daily inventory to reflect upon things I, as a teacher, could have done differently, etc. However, the angels from heaven definitely drove me back to our little house south of Harrisburg that evening. My mind was trying to visualize what had occurred during Jonna's 2:15 meeting at the college. Well, need I say that about ten different scenarios played continuously in my mind within that time frame of thirty-five minutes? Well, need I also say that none of these screenplays even held true?

As I crossed over one solitary little highway hill before approaching Spring Valley Road, I saw the glimmer of the setting sun mirroring off of Jonna's red truck. Suddenly, I felt the rhythm of my heart start racing and excitement caused my pretty stable blood pressure to rise. My Pontiac Grand Am wasn't moving toward our little cedar-sided house fast enough, so I helped gain a little speed by pushing the accelerator all the way to the floor just long enough to have to apply the brakes so I could turn into the driveway. Quickly I gathered up whatever had accumulated upon the passenger seat—purse, grade book, chips, soda, and newspaper. Without tripping over the driveway gravel or baby kittens that were scoping out newly found rocks and bugs, I ran to the door, opened it, and yelled, "Jonna! Where are you?"

I knew perfectly well where she was. Beyond a shadow of a doubt, I knew she would be on the phone with her best of friends telling him what had happened at the college.

Was I right? Yep. Even though I didn't know the specifics of the afternoon's adventure, I did know that the Lord had given her the confirmation she sought. In other words, without being told, I knew where she was going to attend college.

How did I know? Well, let me say, that as her mother, I could hear the excitement in her not-so-quiet voice. I could feel the happiness within her spirit, and I recognized that beautiful glow around her signaling that she was indeed anointed by the Spirit of God. Again, I pondered this moment in my heart and waited patiently for her to finish her phone conversation so I could hear all the details of how God's glory shone that afternoon.

Chapter Twenty-Nine

The Softball Confirmation

NOT LONG AFTER I began to prepare dinner for the day, I heard the sound of a familiar voice coming from Jonna's bedroom telling someone goodbye.

It's not that I was eavesdropping or anything, but I suppose the keen gift that God gave mothers to always be able to listen for our baby's voice, no matter what we were doing, was paying off. Amidst the sounds of banging pots and pans in the kitchen, I could still decipher the words that Jonna was speaking over the phone. No sooner than I heard those words, I heard the distinct sound of feet moving over the carpeted floor. *Here she comes*, I remember thinking.

I stopped whatever dinner chore I was doing at that moment and looked up to see Jonna's beaming face. It wasn't hard to recognize exactly what that radiating beam was for. I walked just a few steps toward that beautiful smile and opened my arms just in time to feel loving arms wrap themselves around me. "Momma, Jesus gave me his answer today. I am going to take the scholarship."

I listened as Jonna's words began to flow. Even with my eardrums fine-tuned and even though I tried desperately to remember everything that my elated baby was telling me that evening, I couldn't begin to catch it all. There have been many times in the past thirteen years that I have tried to recall her words from my memory bank, but all attempts have been futile. Between the excitement she felt and the outpouring of emotion, I simply couldn't. The task was too great, as there was an overabundance of sharing.

However, I absolutely do recall the gist of the one-sided conversation. In a nutshell, the Holy Spirit was present within the four walls of the scout's office that afternoon. Jonna related how, at first, the meeting was strictly academically-based. Their discussion was on a variety of class choices that would be an asset toward Jonna's intended profession of a child psychologist. Next, attention turned to the extracurricular activities that the junior college offered.

In other words, he tried to convince her that the statistics showed that the benefits of an eighteen-year-old attending a junior college far outweighed the benefits of moving away from home and indulging immediately into the full-swing life at a major university. Of course, having attended this particular junior college ourselves, her dad and I had already covered this aspect. I recall that her expressions while dictating this part of their conversation were matter-of-fact and without emotion. Needless to say, these expressions were short-lived. I began to notice a glint of light start to emerge from her eyes as she entered into the topic of the true business of the day.

When the discussion of academics was completed, the next course of action was the trip down a more exciting road of softball. Jonna knew, as well as the scout, that academics were of no importance. She was secure in her knowledge that she was well-prepared for any educational challenges that were surely to be encountered and confident that if she wasn't academically ready for college-level classes that she would just have to study a little harder. I realize that what I just wrote borders on what some would call "cocky" or "conceited"; however, she was neither. Jonna simply had an innate knowledge of what she could do. Yes, this is the same child that just a short while ago was in tears because "nobody likes me." Although I was very grateful for the difference I was seeing in Jonna, my momma instincts were still on alert. I felt this was only covering up the issues that had been causing so many tears.

While I was a child trying to grow up, I was so insecure with myself and my abilities that I missed out on living. The only thing that I knew I excelled at was taking my emotions out on a piano keyboard. Believe me when I say this was a daily occurrence, too. As I was a child in a dysfunctional environment, there were emotions bottled up within the minds of a young girl that should never have been dealt from the stack of cards given her. The result was issues that I am still trying to overcome.

When I delivered my first born, Danny, at age nineteen, I made a resolution that I tried to hold on to as best that I could. I resolved to make sure that he and future children would not mature thinking they were failures. I would often hear the words "I can't" filter from Danny's mouth and later from Jonna's young years. I suppose those words would infuriate this momma faster than any other words my children spoke. In fact, the words "I can't" were simply not acceptable to me because I knew my children could do whatever was required.

To sum up my statement that Jonna was neither "cocky" or "conceited" is simply the fact that she was self-confident in all she endeavored to do. This young lady had no tolerance for anything less than perfection from herself, even though she realized that perfection was not possible to achieve as a human being. She had a deeply-rooted knowledge that her strength and abilities only came from her Lord God. In fact, she would often compare herself to the Apostle Paul because he told in Scripture that as long as he stayed close to the Lord Jesus, he would receive all the heavenly strength needed to accomplish whatever was asked of him.

> And Jesus said unto me, "My grace is sufficient for thee; for my strength is made perfect in weakness." Most gladly therefore will I rather glory in my infirmities, that the power of Christ may rest upon me. Therefore I take pleasure in infirmities, in reproaches, in necessities, in persecutions, in distresses for Christ's sake: for when I am weak, then I am strong.

> 2 Corinthians 12:9–10

This young lady was a perfect example of this Scripture. Jonna was bold, strong, and confident; yet, within her spirit she was compassionate, meek, and humble—giving all glory to her Savior, the Lord Jesus Christ.

But, on the other hand, let's get back to the road of softball. Jonna's big brown eyes only grew bigger and turned browner as she told me the school's offer to her. "Momma, they are going to pay for *everything*." By the time she got to the word "everything," she was shouting with enthusiasm. She said that she couldn't believe the words that were coming out of the school's softball representative. "But that's not all, Momma! You should have been there to hear what he said!" Evidently the scout was definitely interested in her catching skills behind home plate, her batting ability which made a softball soar through the air, her speed in retrieving a caught ball from her glove and easily throwing a runner out trying to steal second base, and her quickness to realize what was getting ready to happen on the field before it actually did.

However, the ability that the scout saw in Jonna the day he met her had nothing to do with softball at all. What he saw displayed in Jonna was a characteristic that only a manager, coach, or scout would even have a sharp-enough eye to notice. His eyesight led him deep into the soul of my baby. He was attracted to the young catcher because of her care and compassion toward the other players. These traits allowed Jonna to keep the pitcher on task, prevented the entire team from falling apart, and produced a team that wasn't composed of nine individual players but a team of nine players that played as one. That was the character that radiated from Jonna that day. That was the character that awarded her a full-ride scholarship. Yep, that was *my* Jonna.

As I recollect, that was the heart of their meeting as far as the softball scout was concerned. But for Jonna, the conversation had just begun. I wasn't there, and I don't really know exactly how she managed to maneuver the topic of a softball scholarship offer into a discussion centering on the spiritual life of the man sitting in front of her. I can only imagine that she saw or felt something within this man's spirit that gave her a green light on approaching the topic of having a spiritual walk with Jesus.

Whatever prompted the change in subject matter, the chairs within that office were occupied by two people who shared a kinship, a bond, and a faith in the Lord Jesus. Stories were exchanged of families, of faith, and of spiritual encounters.

"There were times that I got Holy Ghost bumps while we talked," she told me. "Momma, that was my confirmation that the Lord was going to show me. That's why I agreed to the deal. We are supposed to sign the contract on Friday, May 4, and you and dad have to be there."

After hearing this date, I walked to the calendar to write the appointment in the little square marked May 4, 2001. When I finished writing, I noticed that Jonna had already gone into her room, picked up the receiver on her phone, and had an on-going conversation with an unknown-to-me friend.

After dinner that night, we continued rehashing the day's events, the emotions Jonna was feeling, and the Holy Spirit's involvement in the day. When I felt sleep trying its best to shut my eyes at the same time I was trying to keep them open, I decided to call it a day. I tucked in my angel, kissed her goodnight, and told her that I loved her. As a conclusion to our nighttime ritual, I heard my baby's voice call, "Good night, Momma. I love you," as I walked down the hallway to bed.

Chapter Thirty

Good Friday

It was April 13, 2001, and the morning was beautifully decorated with a fiery orange color streaking across the robin's-egg-blue sky. As I looked out of the bedroom window, I realized there were just a few glimpses of cherry red that helped adorn the majesty of God's palette of color.

Immediately, a thought came to my remembrance, "This is Good Friday. This is the day that my Lord Jesus was crucified on the cross to save me."

With tear-filled eyes that soon overflowed down my cheeks, I turned to walk down the dark hallway to assume my morning chores. Jon was already clocked at work for the early-morning shift, and I heard Jonna's alarm going off, signaling the start of a new morning for her.

She and I were on spring break from school; therefore, the mornings were not as rushed as usual. This school-free week had been filled with spring cleaning, grocery shopping, washing windows, cleaning carpets, and all housewife activities that are only accomplished when the housewife isn't at work. Jonna was working longer shifts that usual at her feed-store job. She didn't mind because she wasn't attending school this week, but I had begun to notice that the long hours were wearing on her. As she waddled into the kitchen that morning, I mentioned that maybe a nap was needed when she got home from work.

My independent eighteen-year-old smiled and proceeded to tell me that her hours had been changed. To my displeasure, I heard, "Momma, they asked me to work longer today. I am going to close."

Well, the momma instinct in me boldly announced that she should call in sick and rest today. Here I am trying to convince my baby to lie.

Now, what kind of example was that? I knew I shouldn't have said those words just as soon as they popped out of my mouth.

"I can't do that," Jonna corrected me. "If I called in, someone else would have to work in my place. It's Easter weekend and they might have plans. I am not sick. I am going to work."

I expected no less from her, I just thought her "tiredness" justified a day off. As I watched her pull out of the driveway and head for work, I said my usual prayer, "Dear Lord, she's so tired. Please let your angels drive with her this morning. Please take care of my baby." With that being said, I turned from the window and proceeded with my scheduled activities for the day.

The day progressed smoothly. My hubby called to tell me that his coworker had called in sick, and he was working a double shift. Jonna called around lunchtime to tell me she was okay, and that she would be home right after work. With a sigh of relief, I continued my chores knowing that she would be home by 10:00 p.m. and could get a good night's rest. Since I was the only one that was going to eat dinner here tonight, I decided to fix my favorite one-skillet dish of hamburger, tomatoes, and Worcestershire sauce. Yes, I do understand that my taste buds can be a bit off balance. At least, that's what others tell me.

As soon as dinner dishes were washed and put away, I sat down in my rocking chair, opened my Bible, and read Jesus' prayer in the Garden of Gethsemane immediately before he was arrested. Of all the prayers that were penned in Scripture, that is my favorite. First, because it is perhaps the most gut-wrenching and most sincere prayer recorded. Secondly, Jesus' words display a unity of his heart, mind, purpose, humility, and self-denial.

> Yes, he prayed for himself: "O my Father, if it be possible let this cup pass from me; nevertheless not as I will, but as thou wilt."

Matthew 26:39

> He prayed for his disciples: "I pray for them: I pray not for the world, but for them which thou hast given me; for they are thine."

John 17:9

After reading this Scripture, I couldn't help but think about all the emotions Jesus must have been feeling at that time. My Lord Jesus, who was about to be arrested . . . wasn't thinking of himself. Even though the humaneness of "fear" surely would have been flowing deeply within his spirit, he was thinking of me. He was giving himself up voluntarily to the Roman soldiers. But to think that my Lord Jesus, who was about to be arrested, beaten brutally beyond recognition, mocked, laughed at, scourged—a Roman form of torture where a victim was lashed repeatedly by a whip composed of several leather thongs with bits of iron or bone attached. The blows were put onto the body by two men, one whipping the victim from one side while another sent lashes from the other side. This led to his eventual crucifixion, and it brings tears to my eyes two thousand years later. Yes, my Savior knew the brutal path of physical and emotional pain he was about to walk down. Even at that, the only begotten Son of God, who cried tears of blood because of his agony, thought of me.

> Neither pray I for these alone, but for them also which *shall* believe on me through their word; that they all may be one; as thou, Father, art in me, and I in thee: that they also may be one in us: that the world may believe that thou has sent me . . . Father, I will that they also, whom thou has given me, be with me where I am; that they may behold my glory, which thou has given me: for thou lovest me before the foundation of the world.

John 17:20–24 (KJV)

As I read this Scripture, I meditated on how important the disciples and the saints of the future actually were to Jesus that night. I remember thinking about the torture my Father must have endured when he turned his back as his Son hung upon that cross gasping for breath. How could anyone possibly turn away from their child when only a spoken word would have saved him? How could a momma stand and watch her first-born son suffer in ways that I could only imagine in a nightmare?

Yet Mary, mother of Jesus, stood nearby and never left her son. Why did this happen? Why was it necessary? This was God's perfect plan for his Son to voluntarily give up his own life. It was the fulfillment of the prophecies of more than eight thousand years ago. It was the only way that I could be allowed to enter the gates of heaven and live eternally with my Father and my Savior.

Jesus became my sacrifice, my perfect sacrifice. Hallelujah! Death no longer had victory! Death was defeated! God's perfect plan was unveiled. By the way, by "death" I don't mean physical death.

We all face a demise of our physical body. However, if we acknowledge our sins before Jesus, repent of them, and believe that Jesus is our Lord, upon physical death, our spirit immediately goes to be with Jesus. In other words, our body is just our house. Our spirit is who we are, and our spirit faces no death—no separation from our Father.

> For God so loved the world that he gave his only begotten Son, that whosoever believeth in him should not perish but have everlasting life. For God sent not his Son into the world to condemn the world; but that the world through him might be saved.

John 3:16–17

As I sat in my rocking chair and continued to think about what Jesus had sacrificed for me long ago, I was unaware that time was slipping by faster than what I had believed. The quietness of our house on Spring Valley Road had provided me a time of uninterrupted reading and praying. My hubby, who was cocooned within the snuggly covers of our bed, would occasionally send a strange snoring sound traveling throughout the house.

At that, Jon wasn't the only quiet one. Casper, our oldest cat, was cuddled on the bed next to Jon's feet. He was our "guard cat," and would definitely let us know if a strange sound filtered into his eardrums.

Then there was Cricket, Jonna's cat, who was sprawled across Jonna's pillow contently sleeping; only to be awakened when she felt Jonna wiggle under the covers. Now, how do I describe Mozart? Well, Mozart was my kitty. Long, yellow hair and spoiled beyond belief. He was the product of Cricket and a male cat that had long yellow hair. Mozart was extremely temperamental and unpredictable, much like the composer he was named after. Mozart didn't stray very far from me, so at that time, he was wedged in between the side of the chair and my legs. Believe it or not, Jon wasn't the only one of God's creation that was snoring, either.

As the serene and peaceful house had provided me with more than adequate Bible study time, it had also given a tranquility which made my eyes grow heavy under their burden of sleep. After noticing that I, too, had evidently been visited by the sandman, I turned toward the wall clock to see if it was anywhere close to 10:00.

I knew that to be the time to look for Jonna's truck to pull into the driveway. Suddenly, my eyelids weren't requesting to be shut. In less time than it took for the second hand on the clock to travel from one number to the next, I was wide awake and filled with alarm. The clock on the wall displayed 10:45, and my baby wasn't home.

Occasionally, there had been other nights that she was an hour or two late, but those nights didn't bring anxiety to my very spirit because she always called to say "Momma, I am okay. Be home later."

But, there had been no phone call, at least not yet. I decided to stay up a little while longer. I walked into the TV room, pulled the afghan off the back of the recliner, picked up Mozart, and sat down to await the head lights of Jonna's truck lighting up the room. Fifteen minutes. Thirty minutes. Forty-five minutes. One hour sped by. It was now midnight, and I had heard nothing from my precious little girl.

Well, the still, small voice in my head was trying to let me know she was fine. However, the momma voice in my head was definitely working double-time. It was the latter voice that was saying, "What if . . . ?" Not only were those words not enough, then I would hear, "What if . . . ?" No matter what words my brain was manufacturing at that time, my gut was trying to fight off the words by telling me everything was all good. Being a woman of faith, I chose to believe my gut and decided to try to go to bed.

If I could just sleep for a little while, Jonna would wake me up when she got home. Of course she would, right?

I didn't want to disturb Jon as he was extremely worn out from the double shift he labored through that day. So, I walked into Jonna's bedroom, pulled down the bedspread, climbed into bed, pulled up the covers, and felt Cricket proceed to nestle under the covers with me.

Not to my surprise, just as we had gotten situated, Mozart pounced on the bed, and the last sound I heard before drifting off into some kind of sleep was Mozart's purr.

Much to my surprise, when I woke up two hours later, there was no Jonna. "Okay. Enough is enough!" I told myself as my Momma's instinct kicked into high gear. I pushed back the covers and the cats, climbed out of bed, and headed to the kitchen in a panic.

"What do I do now?" was my only thought. Without much thought as to whom a phone call would disturb at 3:00 a.m. in the morning, I tugged the phone book out of its drawer, began looking up phone numbers of Jonna's friends and didn't hesitate to dial the numbers of her friends. One voice after another relayed the same message into my ear. "No, Jonna isn't here. I don't know where she would be," the voices said. With each passing phone call, my heart raced faster and faster, and my imagination suddenly produced the most creative scenarios that could be imagined.

Finally, resisting the urge to call the police and the hospitals, I took a deep breath and dialed one last number. I don't understand my logic most times, and in hindsight, I can't honestly say why I didn't call Jonna's best friend's house first. I just didn't. Well, I didn't wake up the entire household with that phone call. I remember one ring, maybe two, and I heard the words, "Hello."

Upon hearing the familiar voice, I said, " . . . Is Jonna there?" Can you imagine how relieved I was when over the phone lines came the word "Yes." After the adrenaline had rushed out of my body, I sat in the kitchen chair and politely asked if I could talk to her. The response was, "She's asleep."

Without thinking that maybe the best thing for her to do was stay there, sleep through the night, and come home in the morning, I blurted out, "Wake her up!" The silence over the phone allowed me a few moments to calm down. I inhaled and exhaled a few times, but I was interrupted by my baby's voice, "Hi, Momma."

We talked long enough for me to discover that Jonna had left work at 9:00 with all intentions of driving her little red truck to our house on Spring Valley Road. But, as we all know, intentions don't always play out the way we intend. A spur-of-the-moment decision to stop at her friend's house before coming home interfered with all intentions. After arriving, the two decided to watch a movie. Jonna's intention was to call and tell me where she was, but that didn't work out according to plan, either.

Because Jonna's day had begun early at school and ended late at work, once she relaxed on the couch beside her best friend, my little sleepyhead nodded off in the comfort of her friend's living room. Because he knew that Jonna was worn to a frazzle, he let her sleep with no plans to wake her so she could make the drive home.

Even though it was so late, I had been frantic with worry because I couldn't find her. I knew I should have let her stay where she was and go back to sleep, but I wanted her to go ahead and make the thirty-minute drive home to Spring Valley Road. In the back of my mind, I had decided that she would be just fine during her trip as she and I talked on the phone. She wasn't reluctant to start home. Of course, by the time our phone conversation had ended, she was awake. My last words to her were, "Call me when you get to the truck!" Compared to the hours that had already passed, the few minutes I waited for the phone to ring was nothing. About ten minutes later, as soon as I heard a ring, I picked up the phone to hear, "Momma, I am on my way home."

During the entire forty-five-minute drive home, we talked over the phone. It was my intention to keep her talking so she wouldn't go to sleep while driving. *That* intention played out, and we chatted until her truck had pulled into the driveway and the engine was shut down in rest.

As soon as my baby walked upon the porch, I opened the door, grabbed her, and hugged her so tightly that neither one of us could breathe. After that, we walked together through the living room, I tucked her into the bed where Cricket was still anticipating her momma's arrival, and turned to go join Jon and Casper in the warmth of my own bed. Exactly on schedule, as I neared the halfway point of the hallway, my ears once again heard my baby's familiar voice saying, "I love you, Momma!" This night, more than any other time, those words filled my heart with thankfulness. Without hesitation, I replied, "I love you, too, baby girl. I will see you when you get up."

It didn't take but a few steps more for me to reach my destination, pull the covers back, climb into bed, and relax to the sounds of my hubby's snores and Casper's purrs.

I prayed, "Thank you, Lord Jesus, for taking care of my little girl. Thank you for bringing her home safely. Thank you for taking my place all those years ago because you loved me. Thank you. I love you, Lord Jesus."

As I drifted off to sleep, I thought about the Scripture I had read several hours earlier. I once again thought of how many tears my Father must have cried and how much his heart must have torn apart as he watched his Son sacrifice his life for a world of sins.

"I could never do what you did, my Father. I could never make it. I couldn't give my babies for someone else," and as I was talking to my Father, my words began to fade, my thoughts turned into dreams, and I slept.

Chapter Thirty-One

Resurrection Sunday

TWO DAYS LATER, RESURRECTION Sunday, I opened my eyes to find the morning sunshine penetrating through the half-opened curtains. As I lay in bed looking through the curtains, I noticed the buds on the various kinds of trees which lined the creekbed which ran alongside our property on Spring Valley Road.

I had been watching the bulging baby leaves daily in anticipation of their blooming; however, it seemed that overnight they had developed a new appearance. In order to inspect them a little clearer, I quietly rolled out of bed so that I wouldn't disturb the slumbering trio that still clung on to early-morning sleep.

As I walked to the window to observe the beauty of this Resurrection morning, my thoughts sprang to life. "Lord Jesus, thank you for this beautiful morning. Thank you for what this morning represents. If you hadn't risen from the dark, lifeless tomb and come back to life, there would have been no hope for me to ever have forgiveness and eternal life.

"Did you know you were going to come back to life as you hung mercilessly upon the cross? Of course you did! That was the plan all along. Christy, you can ask the dumbest questions. Lord Jesus, I know you must sit upon your throne and get so tickled at me. But that's okay. You know me better than anyone else. After all, you made me. I just want to tell you thank you for everything you have done for me and everything that you do for me. Happy Easter, Lord Jesus!"

After thanking my Jesus for the blessings he had given me and scanning the newly-born baby leaves on the trees outside my window, I looked back at my sleeping guys who were still snuggly wrapped up in the covers. My steps guided me down the hallway, and within a few moments I peeked into Jonna's still-dark room.

Her room was on the other side of the house and didn't receive the morning sun. Because she had closed the curtains the night before, I had to take a couple of steps toward her bed to make sure she was sleeping peacefully. I know, I am sure every momma who is reading this makes sure her babies are okay during their nightly slumber. Yep! My angel was sound asleep, and it was my intention to let her sleep as long as possible.

"Lord Jesus, thank you for my Jonna. Please give her strength to keep up the pace she has been running. Please protect her and keep her healthy. You know what happens when she is run down. Please wrap your arms of protection around your child."

Another prayer? Yes! I firmly believe that there is no particular time to talk to my Jesus. I talk to him throughout the day just as though he was standing right next to me.

Having said a prayer of protection around my baby, I headed toward the kitchen to prepare my morning coffee. As the coffeemaker produced its final sound of spewing steam, I grabbed my cup, poured the coffee, and decided to sit in the confines of my screened-in porch.

I understood that the early morning sun wasn't awake enough to warm the chill in the air, but that didn't stop me from the enjoyment of watching the robins bounce across the yard in hopes of finding a nibble of fresh worms that were beginning to stick their wobbly heads out of the ground for a peek at the new day.

Before my venture outside that morning, I reached down and retrieved my journal from its resting place on the table. After a few sips of warm coffee and a few glances at the birds and squirrels gathering food in the yard, I opened my journal and read these words:

> Faith has nothing to do with feelings, or with impressions, with improbabilities, or with outward appearances. If we desire to couple them with faith, then we are no longer resting on the word of God because faith needs nothing of the kind. *Faith rests on the naked word of God.* When we take him at his word the heart is at peace.

God delights to exercise faith, first for blessing in our own souls, then for blessings in the church at large, and also for those without. But this exercise we shrink from instead of welcoming. When trials come, we should say: "My heavenly Father puts this cup of trial into my hands, that I may have something sweet afterwards."

Now the nearer we come to this in our inmost souls, the more ready we are to leave ourselves into his hands, satisfied with all his dealings with us. And when trial comes, we shall say:

> "I will wait and see what good God will do to me by it, assured he will do it." Thus we shall be an honorable testimony before the world and thus we shall strengthen the hands of others."

—George Mueller

No sooner than had my eyes finished scanning these words, the Holy Spirit brought to my remembrance the words Jesus had spoken to me through prophecy last November. In case you have forgotten the prophecy given to me, let me remind you:

> You will face a great tribulation. If you keep your eyes upon me and not look to the left or the right, you will be okay.

Do you remember them now? As the voice of the Holy Spirit brought them to my attention that Resurrection morning, I recalled the words I had just read in my journal which said "Faith rests on the naked word of God!" Suddenly, my heart was heavy. What if I don't have enough faith to go through a tribulation? What if it's bigger than what I can handle? What if the prophecy is wrong and nothing is going to happen? Yeah, what if . . . ? What if . . . ?

These soul-penetrating thoughts didn't last very long. Almost as quickly as Satan produced them in order to weaken my faith, the Holy Spirit boldly said, "Jesus is your strength. Wait patiently in him. Stand firmly on *his words* for no other words are important."

In an instant, the strength and faith which the Lord Jesus had produced within me for the last six months returned. Once again, I *knew* that whatever the tribulation, it was indeed coming!

Once again, my spirit was renewed with unwavering faith and trust in the Lord Jesus. Once again, I *knew* my faith in my Savior would sustain me through whatever was coming to cross my path. Without any hesitation, my prayer language was *boldly* pouring out of my spirit, and I interpreted it as it was spoken.

"The word is God and in *it* I will dwell." Whoa!

As Satan had tried to weaken my stance, Jesus rescued me from the fiery darts that were being thrown in my direction. As my mind was recovering from an "experience of the God kind," I picked up my journal and my empty coffee cup and proceeded into the warmth of the house.

"Lord Jesus, thank you for taking care of me. I don't know what I am getting ready to face, but I know that you are with me through thick and thin. I know that your word says that you will never leave me nor forsake me. Thank you for not letting me be like this empty coffee cup. Thank you for keeping me full. Holy Spirit, thank you for living in me. I love you!"

Upon saying these words to my King of Kings and the Holy Spirit who was sent to me, I noticed that whatever fear might have been instilled within me for a time had vanished.

I also felt an urgency to look at the clock to see the time of day. Just as I thought! Sunrise service will begin all too soon! Even though the task of waking up the Shackleford household was next on my morning's agenda, the spiritual encounter I had just experienced Resurrection morning, 2001, nestled within the walls of my memory . . . a thing never to be forgotten.

Chapter Thirty-Two

Spirit Glowing

As Easter Sunday faded into the past, the next morning's sunrise dawned a new day. As the schools were closed one more day, the day progressed on a calm, peaceful schedule. I proceeded to finish the household chores that were written on the family calendar.

Due to the fact that this was the last vacation day for the break, the duties listed were just about exhausted, but as usual, I had written the ones that I enjoyed the least at the bottom of the list. So, as the morning was unfolding into the latter hours, I had no choice but to honor the undone list and commence with my work. First was the refrigerator.

I never have figured out why I don't like cleaning the "icebox." (I am dating myself because that's what we called the refrigerator when I was a little girl.) I just never did like taking everything out of it and putting it back it. Oh, well! It's true that a woman's work is never done.

As I pulled up a little stool and began to empty the shelves of the refrigerator, I heard familiar sounds coming from the other part of the house. Jonna was awake. I realized that we hadn't discussed any of her plans for the day. I started hoping that she was going to rest some since she had neither school nor work. I continued working on my task at hand until I heard, "Morning, Momma. Whatcha doin'?" softly spoken from my baby. I turned my head to see a naturally beautiful young woman standing in the reflection of the sunshine that was beaming through the kitchen window. I noticed the beauty of her spirit glowing around her as soon as I glanced in the direction in which she was standing.

"Just trying to finish up today," I replied. "What are you gonna do today?" I asked. Much to my relief, she said that her intentions were to just hang around the house for a while. She implied that going back to bed was definitely a possibility. "Good, you need some extra rest," I said in a motherly voice.

With that being said, Jonna retrieved a glass from the cabinet, found the orange juice jug amidst the stash of refrigerator items now located on the floor, filled the juice glass, and quickly gulped down the juice. By this time, Cricket had found her way into the kitchen to see what was going on. However, it didn't take but a few minutes for her to become bored with the activity of cleaning, so after sniffing her way around the kitchen, she vanished into the living room.

Jonna's next move was one that I was relieved to see. Out of the corner of my eye, I noticed that she had walked into the living room, snatched Cricket up into her loving arms, headed for her bedroom, and shut the door. "Thank you, Lord, for telling her to go back to bed. She needs the rest."

After muttering that small prayer, I resumed my task of refrigerator maid. Finally, after finishing, I decided to go check on Jonna. I cracked her bedroom door just enough to allow me to see two things. The first glimpse of movement I saw was Cricket raising her head to see why the bedroom door was opening.

But as soon as she realized there was nothing to fear, her head quickly returned to its nesting place on the covers. My angel baby had gotten back into bed, pulled the snuggly covers around her, and was sound asleep. As I watched her sleep for a few moments, the love I had for her kindled a warm fire within my heart. "Thank you, Lord Jesus, for my precious baby girl," came out of my mouth with no premeditation. Knowing that she was sleeping again, I quietly shut the door and went back into the kitchen. Next on my agenda was washing the windows, but that could wait a little bit because for the next few minutes, I sat in the rocking chair and thanked my Jesus for *everything* he had given me. I meditated on the ways that my Jesus had taken care of me the forty-four years I had dwelled on this earth.

I realized that of all the ways he had blessed me, there were two (other than my salvation) that shined above all—my husband and my babies. As I sat there contemplating how undeserving I was to be so blessed, the Holy Spirit brought forth a Scripture:

> Trust in the Lord, and do good; so shalt thou dwell in the land, and verily thou shalt be fed. Delight thyself also in the Lord; and he shall give thee the desires of thine heart. Commit thy way unto the Lord; trust also in him; and he shall bring it to pass.

Psalm 37:3–5

Once again, my heart filled with peace and love penetrating straight from the heart of Jesus. How could I possibly deserve his almighty love and forgiveness? Well, I didn't, but because Jesus loves unconditionally, I received it every moment of every day. If you have ever been full of this kind of anointment from the Holy Spirit, you will understand that I didn't want to do anything except just sit and be with my Jesus. But, after a little while, I came back to reality and realized there was still work to do at 35 Spring Valley Road.

Hesitantly, I closed my Bible, returned to the calendar on the refrigerator, and proceeded to my next chore on the list. For the rest of the morning, I cleaned and pondered on the words, "He will give thee the desires of thine heart." I was elated, blessed, and joyful. Later in the morning hours, however, I heard the words, "Your tribulation is at hand. Keep your eyes on me. Do not turn to the left or to the right and you will be alright." At first, I tossed the blame of disrupting my joy in Satan's direction, but I soon realized that it wasn't the low-life fallen angel's fault.

The disturbing words were coming from the Holy Spirit in his attempt to once again remind me that no matter what this "tribulation" was that Jesus had my back. Finding the words to say "thank you" for whatever was going to happen sometimes were difficult because I was human, but I was a human filled with the power of the Holy Spirit. Because of this, any fear that I might have possessed back in November had dwindled to such a minimal amount that I didn't notice it at all.

"Okay," I thought, "It's okay! Jesus, I know that you know the road ahead of me. I know that you are with me, and that's *all* I need to know. I can handle whatever lies before me. You will not give me more than I can handle. I thank you, and I love you so much."

Well, I could have gone all morning and not heard that, but I realized that the Lord was just trying to make me stronger. After nearly six months of being reminded of this, my spiritual strength had gotten so strong that I believed I could face Satan and spit in his face. I knew that my faith had grown, my knowledge of the word had increased, my personal relationship with Jesus was beyond what I could ever have imagined, and the power of the Holy Spirit within me was growing day by day.

Yet, after all the time that had gone by and no "tribulation" had occurred, I couldn't help but hope that the prophecy I heard and was frequently brought to my remembrance would never show its face to me. I held on to an unsettling calmness that came when I prayed that no matter what the Lord's will was, that I had heard wrong and that nothing other than everyday issues of life would knock at my door.

I knew deep within my spirit that this optimism was nothing more than a shallow dream. I knew because I knew that something was getting ready to cause me hardship, pain, illness, tears, or maybe all of them. Who knew? I certainly didn't understand or try to figure it out. I knew all I needed to—my faith was with the Lord.

Pushing the negative yet so positive thoughts to the back of my mind, I rerouted my thoughts toward making a decision as to what the Shackleford family was to have for dinner that night. I decided on baked spaghetti. Jon and Jonna loved it, and after cleaning all day, it would be an easy dish to make. Upon opening the door of the newly-cleaned freezer, I took out a pound of ground beef, laid it in the sink to thaw, and went about my tasks.

It wasn't very long until I heard Jonna talking to Cricket as she opened her bedroom door. She had been awake long enough to change her clothes, brush her teeth, and put her long chocolate-brown hair into a ponytail. She was wearing a jacket and had her purse over her shoulder which signaled that she was leaving. Before I could ask, she smiled and said that she was going to Wal-Mart and McDonald's.

"Do you want anything, Momma?" she asked as she opened the back door. I politely thanked her, but said that I didn't. "Okay, be back soon," and with that being said, she headed for the truck and drove to town.

A little while later, I heard the truck pull into the driveway. As Jonna opened the door, she didn't say anything and headed for her bedroom. Curiously, I followed her to see if there was anything wrong. The bubbly young woman who left the house earlier was definitely not the quiet and subdued one who just walked through the door.

Jonna told me that nothing was wrong. From this momma's experience, I had learned that when Danny or Jonna told me nothing was wrong and were quiet about it, and then something was up! Even though I knew better, I also knew that Jonna would come to me when she had it sorted out enough to talk.

By this time, the shadows of the sunshine were leaning from the west windows of the house. I always loved the sunsets that were displayed over the field across from our little house in the country. There was a spiritual essence that beckoned my eyes to gaze deeply into the colors of the horizon. It was as if the brilliant blue, red, orange, yellow, and purple hues radiated directly from the gates of heaven.

As I looked out of the window that evening, I felt a shiver travel throughout my body—a chill, a sensation which I recognized immediately. There was only one person whose presence caused this electricity to penetrate my entire being, and I knew immediately that the Holy Spirit had touched me.

"Hum," I thought, "I wonder why he thought I needed a special touch?" I didn't need to ask him, because no sooner had these thoughts escaped from my brain, than I heard the words, "I am with you. Don't be afraid."

See, I told you that sunsets were a spiritual experience for me. However, to set the record straight, every sunset I saw didn't affect me as the one that evening did. Usually, I just see God's fingerprints in them. I said "thank you" to my Jesus for sending his Holy Spirit to live within me, and as I turned from the window to go start dinner, I couldn't help but wonder,

"What was that anointing for?"

As my feet headed instinctively toward the kitchen to start supper, I felt a strong sensation that I wasn't alone. I knew without any doubt that my Jesus was there with me, unseen but felt. There were no words to describe how I was feeling at that moment.

It was a feeling that could only be described by experience. The Presence of the Lord was *so* intense that I truly believed if I turned around, that I would be face to face with my Savior. A little scary? A lot weird? Yes, but all I knew was I was having an "experience of the God kind."

The peace and love that the Lord was sharing with me at that moment was unbelievable. We read in Scripture that Jesus loves and gives peace; however, there are no words to describe the emotions that had come flowing out of my heart. All I could do was praise him, thank him, and love him with the very essence of my spirit. Yes, the Lord Jesus had come to me that evening giving me a gift.

He gave me his strength, love, and peace in quantities which I had never received before. No words were spoken by my King of Kings. No words were necessary as I recognized his glory.

It wasn't long until I was able to distinguish a figure within the now-darkened room. Jonna had heard my words of praise and decided to come see what was happening. When I realized that my baby was standing in the doorway of the kitchen, I became aware of a recognizable glow that was encircling my daughter. Immediately, the tears that had been flowing from my eyes were a thing of the past. Now, fresh tears of happiness were streaking down my cheeks.

No greater joy could have been given to me, Jonna's momma, at that moment. We were sharing Jesus. Our spirits were connected to him right there in the kitchen. Jesus, Jonna, and I were in one accord! For real, not just in essence! But however wonderful the moment was, it ended with the sound of the chimes coming from the clock on the wall.

I suppose that Jesus decided Jonna and I had experienced enough excitement as the atmosphere of the kitchen had returned to normal.

As we were standing there staring at each other, the familiar sound of Jon's truck pulling into the driveway was heard. All I could do was wrap my arms around my baby and squeeze. She responded, "I love you, Momma." But as she turned to go back to her room, I overheard a small voice say, "I love you, Jesus," and a giggle.

With a smile on my face and in my heart, I quickly started cooking dinner. No matter what activities the rest of the night held, I simply couldn't let go of the joy in my heart, nor did I want to. My mind replayed the scene that had been forever etched into its reservoir of memories. The treasured encounter would never be forgotten, and the generous amounts of Jesus' strength, peace, and love he bestowed were forever to be part of me.

As I closed my eyes that night searching for sleep, a prayer of thanksgiving was offered to my precious Savior.

After all, he alone was worthy to be praised.

Chapter Thirty-Three

Love of Musical Culture

As THE SHACKLEFORD GIRLS reluctantly awoke this morning and did our best to push back the covers of the warm, safe, and secure bed which harbored the dreams of the passed night, our steps were labored.

Spring break had drifted by too fast; however, we agreed on one thing: today would usher in the countdown of the school year's end. I supposed all teachers were probably thinking the same thought that morning. A very dear friend once told me that "teaching is a calling." After several years in the profession, I finally realized that this statement was right.

True teachers love their profession, love to see students grow and mature, and love the chaos the passing days can bring. With that being said, let me state for the record that as much as we love our job, we also love the end of each year. Vacation? Yes!

As much as those in the teaching world look forward to yearly summer vacations, there was one group of students who were eagerly awaiting the last day of school with more anticipation than teachers. There were twenty-eight seniors at Crab Orchard High school that were counting down the days until high school graduation that year, and Jonna was one of them. Throughout this school year of 2000–2001, she had shared many ideas with me pertaining to future plans. Jonna was excited about playing softball for the junior college, and she was eager to find out which university the Lord had picked for her to obtain a master's degree in child psychology.

After college graduation, before settling into her career of counseling needy children, she wanted to travel. Many times she would talk of flying to Germany and Austria. Why? If memory will serve, you might remember that Jonna shared a love of music with me. One of the desires of her heart was to go with me to Europe and visit the cities of musical culture.

Those cities that once housed composers such as Johann Sebastian Bach, Wolfgang Amadeus Mozart, Hector Berlioz, and, of course, Ludwig van Beethoven. She would laugh while informing me that the only way she knew of to get me to go was ending our journey at Bonn, Germany. She knew that I always dreamed of walking down the same streets Beethoven traveled on daily.

Yep! That was my Jonna!

She also understood that I didn't like to travel more than a couple of days at a time. She laughed about it, but understood smiles indicated that one day this expedition would indeed take place.

But for now, back to reality. Before an adventure of that extent could occur, there was a senior year to finish, a senior prom to attend, and a summer vacation that would prove to be possibly the best one ever. You see, Jonna and her friends were now eighteen years old and didn't need parental chaperoning. They were in the process of planning some kind of voyage into their newly launched "freedom" that would begin immediately after graduation.

Needless to say, I was a little hesitant about the idea of my baby taking off with her girls friends—all five of them to a strange place with no adult. Even though I wasn't keen on the notion, I knew that the Lord would watch over them wherever they went. Reluctantly, I also understood that there would come a day when this momma had to cut the apron strings, and whether I enjoyed it or not, that day was soon approaching; maybe it had already come. Oh, well, dreams were dreams, and today's agenda only entailed driving back to school after a ten-day break.

Once again, Jonna left the house on Spring Valley Road long before I did. I'm not really sure why she left so early that morning, but before I was half-way ready, she hollered, "See ya at school, Momma," and was out of the door.

I remember wondering where she got her burst of energy all of a sudden. With that thought, I put my actions in gear, finished my daily makeover, grabbed my purse, and headed out of the door. As soon as I shut the car door and turned the ignition key, I said, "Okay, Lord Jesus. Let's go to school," and I was off.

Chapter Thirty-Four

Stillness

THE MORNING'S CLASSES SEEMED to pass with tremendous effort. I supposed it was because my body and mind were trying to readjust to a school schedule once again. I didn't see or hear from Jonna any that morning, so I assumed everything was going well for her. Finally, the lunch bell sounded, and as my fourth-hour junior high choir scampered out of the music room door, I felt myself heave with a great sigh of relief.

The morning was over, the day was half done, and at last I could have a few moments to myself. I decided to go to the cafeteria, fix a salad from the salad bar, come back to my room, and behind a closed door eat my lunch in the stillness of the moment. My music room was hardly ever student-free. Sometimes students would come into the room for a conversation, sometimes they would come in small groups to get away from the lunchtime noise in the gym, and sometimes they just longed for a time of solitude . . . just as I was hoping for.

I didn't mind them coming into my room. In fact, most days I enjoyed it. That was one of my rewards for being a music teacher. Within the bounds of choirs, special bonds were formed and friendships were made. In other words, a choir could be described as a small community of students who share a common goal—a love of music. Because I was allowed the great blessing being part of that community, my students grew to be part of me. However, on that particular day, I just needed to be alone with my thoughts for a while.

For some reason, my request was granted and I was allowed a conversation-free time. Sometimes it's not the best thing to get what we ask for, however. During those forty minutes of solitude, I began to get an uneasy feeling within my spirit. This experience was no stranger to me, though. Ever since the prophecy of a "great tribulation" had been voiced to me six months earlier, I had been visited with a spirit of heaviness frequently. I *knew* that the prophecy was going to come true. I *knew* because the voice of the Holy Spirit kept reminding me that if I kept my eyes on Jesus I would be okay!

But as usual, the only questions I had were: What was the tribulation, and when was it going to happen? Of course, neither one were answered that day.

Suddenly I had to interrupt my lunch and solitude to go to the Lord in prayer. The still, small voice of my Jesus guided me to reach for a devotional book that I kept alongside a Bible on my desk. After taking the devotional into my hands, I asked the Lord to direct my hands to what he wanted me to read. In faith and belief that he would show me, the devotional was opened and the following poem was revealed to me.

The Eye of the Storm

Fear not that the whirlwind shall carry thee hence,
Nor wait for its onslaught in breathless suspense,
Nor shrink from the whips of the terrible hail,
But pass through the edge to the heart of the tale,
For there is a shelter, sun lighted and warm,
And Faith sees her God through the eye of the storm.

The passionate tempest with rush and wild roar
And threatenings of evil may beat on the shore,
The waves may be mountains, the fields battle plains,
And the earth be immersed in a deluge of rains,
Yet, the soul, stayed on God, may sing bravely its psalm,
For the heart of the storm is the center of calm.

Let hope be not quenched in the blackness of night,
Though the cyclone awhile may have blotted the light,
For behind the great darkness the stars ever shine,
And the light of God's heavens, his love shall make thine.
Let no gloom dim thine eyes, but uplift them on high
To the face of thy God and the blue of his sky.

The storm is thy shelter from danger and sin,
And God himself takes you for safety within;
The tempest with him passeth into deep calm,

And the roar of the winds is the sound of a psalm.
Be glad and serene when the tempest clouds form;
God smiles on his child in the eye of the storm.

—Unknown

Wow! I paused any further conversation. I couldn't speak. My lips were paralyzed and my entire being frozen except for the warmth of gentle tears of love for my Jesus dripping down my cheeks. "Thank you, my Jesus!" Those were the only words that I could manage to say. "Thank you, my Jesus!" How could I ever doubt that my Lord wasn't with me? How could I ever believe for one moment that he wasn't really the Son of God? How could I doubt? How could anyone doubt? Once again, when the presence of the Lord allows us an "experience of the God kind," there can be no doubt.

There I sat in awe of the power of my Lord. There I sat motionless. Having no desire to move, speak, or think, there I sat! I don't have any idea how long I sat there relishing in the presence of my Lord. But time has a way of passing too fast, and my meditation was sorely interrupted by the sound of the bell signaling that lunch was over. I soon realized that my salad had gone virtually untouched, and the ice in my tea glass had all but melted.

"Oh, well," I thought. I will just finish eating while my next class files through the door. But as I watched the kids walk into the classroom and hurriedly ate my salad that was wilted by Italian dressing, I couldn't help by chuckle to myself. "I wonder what people would say if they knew that I prayed in my room and was visited by the Holy Spirit?" It didn't matter to me what anyone else thought. In fact, I was blessed with coworkers who would understand exactly what I had just experienced. But as I finished my lunch and desperately tried to revive myself into the physical realm, I could only smile and laugh.

Needless to say, the afternoon went by smoothly. Even though musical terms, definitions, and ideas flowed out of my mouth that afternoon, my inward thoughts kept reflecting back to the poem the Holy Spirit led me to and the peace that my heart felt after reading it. I couldn't wait until school was over that day so I could tell Jonna what had happened during lunch.

All through the drive home that afternoon, I replayed the message from the Lord over and over. I still could only give him praise and thanksgiving for coming to me that day and the days past. My human side tried to worry about the coming tribulation, but my spiritual side *always* overcame any fretfulness. As a result, I continued on living in peace and contentment because I trusted in the Holy Spirit's words "Keep your eyes on Jesus, and you will be okay."

Upon pulling into our driveway on Spring Valley Road, I saw the familiar sight of squirrels playing in the yard and birds digging in the damp spring soil in order to unearth worms for their afternoon snack. This picture produced even more peace in my heart as I remembered the words Jesus spoke to hundreds of people as he sat on upon a mountain two thousand years ago:

> Therefore I say unto you, Take no thought for your life, what ye shall eat, or what ye shall drink; not yet for your body, what ye shall put on. Is not the life more than meat, and the body more than raiment?
>
> Behold the fowls of the air; for they sow not, neither do they reap, nor gather into barns; yet your heavenly Father feedeth them. Are ye not much better than they?
>
> . . . And why take ye thought for raiment? Consider the lilies of the field, how they grow; they toil not, neither do they spin: And yet I say unto you that even Solomon in all his glory was not arrayed like one of these.
>
> . . . Take therefore no thought for the morrow: for the morrow shall take thought for the things of itself. Sufficient unto the day is the evil thereof.
>
> Matthew 6: 25–34 (KJV)

"Lord Jesus, I thank you for bringing this to my remembrance. Whatever you are preparing me for, I know it's your will. Whatever it is, I know you are with me. I will be okay. You, in your wisdom, understand the things that happen on this earth. I trust you with all my heart and all that I am. I know your plan is perfect no matter what. I love you. I thank you for this spring day and for the joy and blessings you have given me today."

I understood only one thing that afternoon: I understood the love the Lord Jesus had for me. The only reason he would make sure that I knew he was with me was because of his forgiving and unconditional love for me. For such a display of love, I was forever thankful.

With this Scripture resting upon my heart and a song of praise upon my lips, I decided that for at least a little while it was time for me to leave my thoughts of the Spiritual things and go into the house to cook dinner for my family. After going through the daily ritual of deciding what everyone else wanted to eat for supper, I finally chose and began preparing the meal. Jon would be home in just a few minutes, and Jonna would follow soon enough. Even though my concentration was on kitchen duties, I still couldn't wait until I could share the day's events with my angel girl.

Chapter Thirty-Five

Path of Confliction

THE EVENING PASSED TOO slowly. It was one of those times when the old adage, "a watched pot never boils," kept coming to my mind. I talked to Jon, sat in my favorite blue reading chair, and anticipated the sound of Jonna's truck pulling into the rocked driveway on Spring Valley Road. After what had seemed to be hours, I heard the sound of crunching rocks outside of the living room window.

Finally!

My baby girl was home, and I could share with her the spiritual encounter of that day.

The discussion that Jonna and I held that night didn't go as planned, however. The minute I saw that beautiful face in the dimmed living room light, this momma understood immediately that the experience I enjoyed so much that day was going to be the least of any words spoken that night. Jonna looked at me, forced a smile which followed with the usual "Hi, Momma," and traced a path of footsteps, leading to her bedroom. No sooner than she had entered her bedroom sanctuary, I heard the door shut.

"Okay, Lord. Let's go see what's going on with my baby," were the words that came out of my mouth as soon I heard the wooden door.

I laid my Bible to the side, got up out of my rocking chair, and headed to her room. Without a knock on the door or a word from my mouth, I opened her door. My heart sank as I discovered my angel girl lying on her bed crying. I didn't take time to ask why she was upset nor did I hesitate to sit down beside her and pull back her thick brunette hair which was covering up her tear-stained face. With only the knowledge of a momma's instinct to comfort her baby, I reached to take Jonna into my arms. There was no effort to hold her, however, for just as soon as I had uncovered her distraught face, Jonna sat up, buried her face within the loving arms of her momma, and cried. The only sound in the room at that moment were the sobs and sniffles from my baby. No words were spoken—not yet.

After a while, she decided to break the bonds of my encircled arms and reach for a tissue. "Momma, I just don't understand," I heard her shaky voice say. I assumed that her lack of understanding had something to do with her boyfriend, a friend, or school. I assumed wrong!

"Momma, I don't know what I want anymore. You know how I always wanted to be a psychologist and help the little kids? I don't know now. I don't know what the Lord is telling me to do. I don't understand why I am so confused. I am so mixed up, and the more I ask Jesus to show me, the more I don't know what he is trying to say. It's like he isn't saying anything. It's like he isn't hearing me, but I know he is. Momma, why isn't he answering me? Have I got stuff all wrong? Have I misinterpreted what he said? Am I even supposed to go to college?"

As I listened to the wavering voice of my confused angel girl, I couldn't help but notice the big tears that had once again started running down her cheeks, causing her to grab hold of her momma as if she were clinging for dear life. I didn't remember the last time this precious angel had held on to me with such a death grip. While she was beneath the shelter of momma's arms, I was silently asking the Lord Jesus for answers. How was I supposed to answer this child? What did she need for me to say?

"Lord Jesus, help me help my baby, your child." Those were the only words that I could say. I was so thankful that I began to speak in the "tongues of angels," because then I knew that the Holy Spirit was speaking to Jesus in my place. I was confident that Jesus was hearing my inner spirit-felt words instead of any words that my mind was fumbling to speak. I sat there on the bed rocking my baby in loving arms, praying for any and all understanding that the Lord would give, and realized that I was still unaware of what the real problem was. I still was ignorant of any facts that led this confident, wise, and mature child of God to be broken. "Okay," I thought, "it's time to find out what is really wrong."

As I tried to pull away from my little girl, she reluctantly let go. "Jonna, now can you tell me what happened to make you feel this way? It will help." There wasn't much she could say. I discovered she had no answer to my question. "Momma, I don't know. I was okay, and then I wasn't. I felt good. I was in a good mood, and then all of a sudden at work,

I started feeling somewhat bad. On the way home, I realized that I didn't know what I wanted anymore. I don't know if I even want to play softball, go to school, and I don't think the Lord wants me to help the little ones. Have you ever felt like the Lord just didn't want to talk to you? Have you ever felt like he wasn't there anymore? *That's* the way I feel. I feel so empty, and I don't know how to fix it."

I responded with every ounce of strength that I could to offer her some positive perspective.

"Sweetheart, you *do* know how. The only thing you need is quiet time with him. Sounds like you have been trying to rush Jesus. Sometimes he needs your undivided attention. Not while you are working or driving. Just you and he time. How many times did I try to quit college because I didn't think I could finish or because I tried to convince myself that the Lord didn't want me to finish? If it hadn't have been for Daddy, Danny, and you, I would have never got my degree. I would have quit because for a time, I didn't hear what Jesus wanted me to do. After many days of driving home from Carbondale with tears in my eyes, I finally realized that I was simply worn out. I had not taken any time to just enjoy the experience. When I didn't try so hard, the experience of going to a university wasn't so bad. You, my dear, are worn out. Between school, softball games, work, and a steady boyfriend, you are exhausted. You don't have to see your boyfriend every night. Let him come here. Sweetheart, you are only one young woman. A beautiful, compassionate, giving one, too. But you have to rest sometimes. Maybe you are getting a little bit nervous. You only have three more weeks until graduation. After that, all the dreams you have had will start to become a reality. Right now, though, I am going to go warm up your dinner so you can eat. Jonna, I love you. You are a beautiful child of God. He isn't ignoring you, I promise. It will be all fine. After graduation, you will have all summer to rest and recoup. I know that Jesus will help you figure it all out."

Upon realizing that my little girl had quit crying and managed a small grin, I left the room to fix the last dinner plate of the night. Even though my heart was breaking because Jonna was hurting, I smiled because I knew Jesus and she would work it out. "After all, we all have times when we feel lost and abandoned. Thank you, Lord, that they are only temporary," I said as I walked to the kitchen. While stacking Jonna's dinner plate full, I couldn't help thinking about my baby girl.

After her plate was ready, I took it to her room hoping she wasn't crying again. As I neared her door, I exhaled a sigh of relief when I heard her talking on the phone. The door was opened, which showed that she was feeling better. I didn't know who was on the other end of the phone conversation, but I found a meager little grin on her face as I delivered the supper plate. My motherly instinct told me that it was probably her boyfriend. When I turned to leave the room, Jonna giggled and mentioned a familiar name. Yep. The educated guess was correct. He could always make her smile.

The hours until bedtime rolled quickly by that night. When my eyes couldn't stay open any longer, the path down the hallway into the waiting bed was way too long. Within the bounds of a dimly-lit hall, I noticed a strange silence penetrating from behind Jonna's bedroom door. My curiosity had to investigate because usually my little night owl was reading, studying, or talking on the phone. Tonight was different. Though the bedroom light was out, the outside vapor light produced enough light that it caused Jonna's bedroom to be vaguely lit. Through the shadows, I could see her snuggled within the covers. For just a few moments, I simply stood there and watched my angel baby sleep. The only reflections that could be seen were the peaceful expression on Jonna's face, and Cricket wrapped securely underneath one of Jonna's arms.

"Thank you, Lord Jesus. Thank you for helping her sleep. She so needs to rest." Having muttered that softly-spoken prayer and being confident that my angel was sleeping, I turned and proceeded to my bed where I knew Jon, Casper, and Mozart were already hibernating for the night. Any confidence that Jonna was sound asleep was shattered as I walked down the silent hallway to bed. The words, "I love you, Momma," resonated within my ear drums. Warmth and love built within my heart, and the words, "I love you, Jonna," echoed back to her. "How in the world did she know I was there? She was sound asleep!" flowed from my mouth.

The words were spoken more to myself than to the Lord, but I heard His comforting voice of assurance proclaim, "Your spirits are connected." Now, tears formed within my sleepy eyes. At that moment, my heart was so filled with love and awe. "My Jesus, thank you. Just, thank you!" As I crawled into the warmth of our bed, Jon had drifted off to sleep, Casper was stretched out along the bottom of the bed snoring, and Mozart had made his bed on the pillow above my head. Knowing that the Shackleford clan was safe and accounted for, thanksgiving filled my heart and love flooded within my spirit. As my thoughts faded, I remember whispering, "I never did tell Jonna about the Lord visiting me today. Oh, well, there's always tomorrow." Then, no more words came. Only sleep.

Chapter Thirty-Six

Tribulations

THE NEXT MORNING DAWNED anew; however, Jonna's countenance was less than her normal bubbly self. We discussed the day's schedules and spoke about different topics over breakfast. As I kept waiting for an open door to tell her of my glorious experience with the Holy Spirit yesterday, I sensed something that was alarming to me. I absolutely knew that Jonna was experiencing turmoil within her spirit that she didn't comprehend. For the first time in this child's spiritual walk with Jesus, he was not answering her questions. I remember thinking that maybe for the first time, Jonna wasn't listening to his answers. Whichever was the right conclusion, it didn't matter. All I knew was my baby girl was going through her own tribulations right now.

My heart ached for her, and I felt her pain. She was enduring the motions of joy, happiness, and peace; yet her spirit was dull and lifeless. There had only been one other time that I remember my angel being so down. It was the Sunday morning the voice of the Holy Spirit asked me to take Jonna's hand and go to the altar with her. If you will remember back a few months ago, the Lord spoke these words to my daughter: "You will touch the lives of thousands."

That simple statement impacted her spirit so greatly that immediately she recovered from her downward spiritual spiral. At this time, my prayer for her was only, "Lord Jesus, please talk to Jonna. Please make sure she hears your voice, and please give her the understanding she needs to work through this tough time she's going through."

I realized that this was only a temporary occurrence for her. As any of my readers who walk with the Lord and hear his voice will confess, we *all* have those times. For whatever reasons, there are times that Jesus just seems so out of reach.

After breakfast was eaten—or picked at that morning—we had to start getting ready for school. I ran late with everything I was attempting to finish as I was desperately trying to keep an eye on my baby girl and earnestly kept repeating "Lord Jesus, please help her." Jonna's actions seemed to be covered with molasses. She was in no hurry to do anything. I was expecting to hear, "Momma, I think I will stay home today." However, the statement wasn't uttered. Finally, I broke the silence and asked her if she wanted to stay home from school and spend the day in solitude and prayer. My answer was, "No. I will be okay."

I wasn't sure how either of us made it to school before classes started, but we did. I wasn't convinced that either of us should have even been there that day. Despite my classes and student discussions, my spirit never left Jonna's. All the while I was teaching and talking, my heart was praying for her. Anticipation within me escalated as lunchtime drew closer. At last, the lunch bell rang. With no hesitation, I grabbed my purse and rushed out of the music room door to find my baby. As I hurried past the congregation of students in the high school hallway, the cafeteria finally came into sight. A deep breath was drawn and released as I looked into the room to see Jonna and her girlfriends engaged in conversation while sitting at their daily lunch table. From a distance, Jonna seemed to be enjoying the company of her friends.

"Whew! Thank you, Jesus, for this blessing," I said not caring if anyone heard me or not. I was so thankful to see the smile on her face, forced or not. I was thankful and relieved. My thought was, "Maybe Jesus and she had worked it out." Even though I was relieved, I wasn't at peace. Something was wrong. Something had not been resolved. Something, but what?

As much as my mind was trying to figure out what was still harboring discontentment within Jonna's spirit, my stomach was hungry. Deciding that I needed to eat, I walked to the salad bar, filled my plate with the delicacies the bar held, walked to the teacher's table, and silently ate.

My afternoon schedule had been amended due to a lyceum being held for the grade school kids. I surely didn't mind having an hour or so to catch up. I made the executive decision, however, to take a break. I thought it would be nice to just walk to the break room, catch up on the school gossip, and chill for a while. As I walked beyond the library door on my way to the teacher's room, I glanced into the library. My heart dropped into my shoes when I noticed Jonna sitting at a computer cubicle, all alone, and crying. Without thought of interrupting anyone, my feet took a deliberately straight path toward my baby. She looked up with her tear-filled eyes as soon as I touched her on the arm and asked her what was wrong. Immediately, the tears in her eyes flowed in streams down her faded cheeks. "Momma," she said, "My life is falling apart. I don't understand."

"Where are you supposed to be right now?" I replied.

After hearing that she was supposed to be in English, but had asked to be excused to go to the restroom, I instructed my baby to go to my room and wait for me. As I walked out of the library, Jonna went down the hallway, and I proceeded up the stairs to talk to the high-school English teacher. I informed him that I needed to talk to Jonna for a few minutes. He told me that she was in the restroom and that she could go with me. I refrained from correcting him and hurried to the music room where she was waiting for me.

I had already said every word of consolation that I knew to say. Actually, I had no idea the true source of Jonna's heartache until a few moments before entering my classroom. It was as if a lightbulb had been turned on inside my brain. Of course! I thought that at that moment I completely understood the problem. So I entered the room and shut the door.

"Jonna, I think I know what to tell you. I truly believe that you are not hearing the voice of the Holy Spirit because your mind is burdened by something else. What is it?"

"Momma, I just feel empty inside. Nothing is as it used to be. Some of my friends have drifted apart. We aren't close like we have always been. I miss that so much. Between that emptiness and the Lord being quiet, I just hurt all inside." As I listened, I knew exactly what she had been talking about. I understood the basis of her emotional upheaval. No wonder my angel was so distraught. It wasn't just a spiritual battle.

"Sweetheart, you are a beautiful young lady. Girls just have ups and downs with friends whether we like it or not. I know that your heart is broken, but people change and move on. They don't forget us, but maybe the Lord changes their direction. Or maybe he's changing your direction, not theirs. Sometimes we just have to accept the things we don't understand and let the Lord give us strength and lead us to whatever path he shows. Changes aren't bad, but I know they can hurt. Hearts are broken, but can be mended. Just remember that 'when the Lord shuts a window, he opens a door.'"

It was then that I noticed my little girl—a woman now—was smiling. I didn't have a clue which spoken words made her tears stop. It didn't matter. My heart danced as her smile indicated that peace had replaced confusion within her spirit. For this I was thankful. As I watched Jonna stand, walk to me, and sit in my lap, I was even more thankful. Tears of joy formed in my eyes as I sat holding my baby. There were tears of happiness that had been shed many times in my life as I had watched my daughter travel through the stages of life. They did so because of the gratitude and pride I had of being her momma. In the background of this priceless and loving moment, the class bell sounded.

"Momma, I gotta go to class. Thank you for being here for me. I love you," Jonna spoke as she walked toward the door. I shut my tear-filled eyes and softly said,

"Thank you, my Jesus, for my precious baby girl."

After taking a few deep breaths, I once again decided to spend the rest of my break relaxing. On my way to the break room, it occurred to me that maybe the great tribulation that was coming was already over. Maybe the pastor was right, and the severity of the tribulation wasn't a big deal. Could it have been some kind of daily struggle that was handled with prayer? Maybe it was something that was kept from getting serious because I looked to Jesus for an answer. Maybe my tribulation had come and gone.

Those maybes brought a smile to my face, but an uncertain feeling within my heart. Now, I was the one with uncertainty. Now, I was the one with hesitation. Now, I was the one wondering. As I continued my trek to guzzle down a Diet Coke from the office, I realized a fear within my spirit. I suddenly realized that I had been carrying this feeling since I heard the words of the prophet concerning a "great tribulation." I realized that even though the Lord had caused me to have a tremendous spiritual growth spurt, that I had ignored any possible sign of being scared.

Now, with no warning, I knew I was a little bit afraid of what may come my way. But, I also was well aware that the Lord Jesus had made me spiritually strong. No matter what, there was one thing and one thing that I knew with no uncertainty: I trusted my Jesus with everything. And no matter what, it would be okay.

Chapter Thirty-Seven

Spiritual Battle

THE NEXT SUNDAY MORNING was a gloriously restful day. I say "restful" because not only was the Shackleford house calm and peaceful that beautifully sunny Sunday, the Holy Spirit had visited our church service that morning and given healings, prophecies, and joy to all who were in his presence. Jonna's boyfriend traveled from Carterville that morning to attend church service, eat dinner, and spend the day with her. I was so thankful that he did. Because she had been through several days of spiritual and mental battles, I was thankful that finally she would enjoy a day of happiness with the boy she was dating.

After the church service that day, the congregation enjoyed a fellowship dinner honoring our pastor and assistant pastor. I had grown up hearing the adage that Southern Baptist women "sure knew how to cook." The dinner prepared by the women of our church put those words to shame. Let me clarify for the record that being charismatic in our faith led us to a variety of churches which believed in the full power of the Holy Spirit and we had eaten many dinners prepared by women of a kindred belief in the powers and gifts of the Holy Spirit. These women, in my opinion, now held the title of knowing how to cook. That Sunday's fellowship dinner bestowed delicacies that were so delicious that we all could safely say we had committed the sin of gluttony. However, as fellowship continued, I kept my eyes on my baby girl and her date. My heart was so overwhelmed by the sadness she had been carrying, and my instincts were on alert to pounce upon anything physical or spiritual that would dare interfere with my baby girl's happiness that day. Needless to say, I was just a tad bit overprotective. The day progressed showing only signs of joy and elation from Jonna's spirit.

I watched with keen spiritual insight as she ate and talked with her church family. After a while, my spirit relaxed enough to enjoy dinner as the only emotion I saw shooting from Jonna's chocolate-brown eyes was happiness as I watched her introduce her boyfriend to various people of the church whom she had grown to love—which was almost all of them. The fiery sparks of joy coming from her eyes could only be compared to sparks from fireworks that illuminate the dark skies on the Fourth of July. As I discerned that my little girl was at peace, I said a quiet prayer of thanksgiving to my Lord Jesus for helping my daughter. Then, with a cautious peace, I enjoyed the rest of the dinner.

As the fellowship dinner closed, goodbyes were said, and the Shackleford family, plus one, headed to Spring Valley Road. Once inside the house, the four of us immediately proceeded to various locations of the house to replace our church attire for more comfortable clothes. It didn't take long for me to gather up laundry, sort it, and put it in the washer. However, within that short period of time, the other three candidates for a nap were already sound asleep. "Wow," I said to whomever was listening, "That didn't take long." With the entire household, including three cats, sleeping, I proceeded into the living room. I reached for a book I had been reading. After opening the book, I laid it in my lap, meditated upon the many blessings that I had received that morning, and within a few moments I had joined my family in dreamland.

Naps have never been my thing. I am guilty of nodding off in my chair; however, the duration of sleep isn't an all-afternoon event. True to that, after just a few minutes, I opened my eyes to find the shadows of the sun lingering in just about the same positions they held when my eyes closed. Immediately, I noticed that the household was still quiet. I got up to investigate whether I was the only one awake, and I was. Jon was still snoring on the couch with Casper lying at his feet. Upon walking a short distance to the hallway, I peeked in the bedroom and found Jonna's boyfriend asleep on the foot of the bed and my angel sleeping peacefully with Cricket under her arms. As I heard the sound of pitter-patters coming across the floor, I detected Mozart following me. After realizing everything was in order, I walked back into the living room to read my book.

The minutes turned into hours, and I heard movement coming from the hallway. The two youngest sleeping beauties had awakened. They were coming into the living room announcing that they were hungry by saying, "What's for supper?"

It was at that moment that I realized it was time to fix something. After all, we had stuffed ourselves only three hours ago. I proceeded to put down my book, head to the kitchen, and prepare something to snack on. Jonna and her boyfriend turned the television on, laughed, and talked while I was in the kitchen. My heart was filled with joy and contentment as I overheard their laughter. At that particular moment, all was right with the world. Momma was in the kitchen, kids were laughing in the other room, and Dad was snoring on the couch. My day was complete.

Dinner consisted of hotdogs and fries. Soon after dinner, Jonna's date announced that he had to leave. Goodbyes were said, and once again the house was quiet. No sooner than he pulled out of the driveway, Jon, Jonna, and I began making preparations for bed. It didn't matter that we had napped that afternoon. Tomorrow was another day, and the start of a busy week.

As I lay on my pillows that night, I heard Jonna's voice echoing from her bedroom. I knew that she was on the phone with someone. It could have been a friend, Danny, or her sister-in-law. I didn't know, and I didn't care. It just felt so wonderful to know that the Lord Jesus had helped her through a few difficult days. With a smile on my face because my angel girl was back to normal, I gave thanks to Jesus for the awesome day he had allowed us to share and for the many ways he blessed me that day. As I felt my eyes struggling to stay open, I closed my prayer and allowed myself to enter into the world of dreams. After all, if everything went according to schedule, next week was going to be a whopper of a week. Never did I realize the size of the whopper it was to be.

Chapter Thirty-Eight

Peace

EARLY THE NEXT MORNING, I awoke to the sound of Jon's alarm ringing. As I noticed no movement from the other side of the bed, I nudged him. Then I nudged him again . . . and again. Finally, he was conscious enough to turn the alarm off. The moment that task was accomplished, snores from the bed infiltrated the quietness of the room.

I knew not to go back to sleep until he was standing on the floor. In fact, the longer I prolonged the final nudge of the morning, the more wide-awake I became. Then, it happened! The last call of the alarm sang out one more time and ten minutes had passed. It was 3:45 a.m., and no more time could be allowed for my hubby to sleep. Rolling over, I pushed him one last time, and said, "Get up, Jon. You have to get up." With that being said and the alarm clock chiming in, he reluctantly opened his eyes, sat up on the edge of the bed, and turned off the alarm. Normally, as soon as he got out of bed, I would roll over, pull the covers around me, and go back to sleep until my alarm interrupted me later.

However, this morning, I realized that I was too awake to comply with my routine. Instead, I headed for the kitchen to make my first cup of coffee.

After Jon left for work, I sat down with my coffee to talk to Jesus and read my morning devotional. I remember thinking to myself that since I had gotten up two hours early that morning, there would be no reason not to enjoy the early morning sunrise. As I sipped the steaming coffee, my mind tried to remember all the tasks that this week held. Today was Monday, and as far as I knew, there was nothing out of the ordinary today. Tuesday's schedule consisted of a regular school day, Jonna's softball game immediately after school, and a dinner that was being held for chosen faculty and students of various schools in southern Illinois.

The students were invited to this dinner based upon academic grades, achievements, and character. Jonna had received her invitation a few days ago. Wednesday was considered a normal calendar day. Then, Thursday was Honor's Day at school and Jonna had a softball game at Crab Orchard. Once Friday came, the schedule really became hectic. Immediately after school on Friday, Jon, Jonna, and I were to meet with the academic heads and the junior college. Jonna was scheduled to sign a contract with the school to play softball next year.

After the signing, it would be official, and she would receive a full scholarship for her first year of college. Jonna was going to stay all night with her friend Friday night to do manicures and pedicures. Saturday morning, the two girls were getting professional hair styles, Jonna would drive home, and Saturday night was her senior prom. Jon and I hadn't decided if we were going to chaperone the prom, but we were invited. Finally, Sunday was going to definitely be a day of rest for the Shackleford family.

As I sat in my rocking chair that morning and thought about the week ahead, I felt a smile growing within my heart and a peaceful feeling arise within my spirit. Yes, my little girl had grown into a beautiful young woman. I was so proud of her accomplishments and so blessed to be her momma. Instantly, my smile turned upside down. The peace I felt had turned into turmoil as I suddenly understood the price I was going to pay because she was no longer my "baby." It was hard for me to realize that my little girl was grown up. It was going to be harder for me to let go of those apron strings. I didn't know if I could cut them loose or not.

I thought back to the day she started kindergarten. I sat in the car and watched her big brother take her by the hand and lead her into the school. I cried major tears that morning because my baby was getting ready to attend her first day at kindergarten. How in the world would I be able to watch her driving off for college? How could I possibly be able to go to bed at night without hearing "I love you, Momma" ring down the hallway? Did I even begin to know how difficult it was going to be not to sit on her bed every night and discuss our days? No, I didn't. In fact, I just decided not to think about it anymore. I knew that I would always have my Jonna close by. She was my kindred spirit—my spiritual sister. I decided that morning that changes were coming, but I would never have to let go of her completely. Our hearts would always be united, and our spirits would always share their love. No, even if Jonna decided to go away to college, she would never completely leave Spring Valley Road. My prayer turned into a determined plea for the Lord Jesus to guide her close to home.

If any of my readers are mommas, you will completely understand the power of a momma's determination, will, and prayers. I heard the words, "Lord Jesus, I know you will lead her according to your perfect will, but please keep her close to home." I believed with all my heart that that was the way it was going to be. I had faith; yet, it was cautious faith because in my heart I knew that the Lord had already paved her footsteps down the road he had chosen for her.

I just hoped I would get my wish, but I knew it wasn't up to me. Not anymore.

Chapter Thirty-Nine

Matthew 6:24

UPON THE REALIZATION THAT I had been bombarded with too many thoughts that morning, I decided to end my thinking for a while. Jon, as well as many people who cared about me, had always said that I think too much. They were all correct, and I knew it. I also knew that my great-grandmother McGuire always said that the things we worry about most were the things that never happened. Through the years, I had found that to be true.

"Okay," I said, "okay, Lord Jesus, I have to get ready for school. Enough is enough. This is going to be a beautiful day," I told myself.

With those words being spoken, I took one final sip of my cooled coffee and proceeded to start getting ready for school. Jonna's alarm hadn't gone off yet, so I began doing morning chores and delayed fixing breakfast until she was awake. I knew she was facing a taxing week and made the decision to let her sleep any chance she got. While getting ready that morning, I heard the voice of the Lord reminding me of a Scripture. I heard his voice telling me to read Matthew 6:24. As I heard him tell me the second time, I laid down the makeup items that were in my hand, went back to my rocking chair, picked up my Bible, and read the Scripture my Jesus was trying to show me.

> Take therefore no thought for the morrow: for the morrow shall take thought for the things of itself. Sufficient unto the day is the evil thereof.
>
> Matthew 6:24

Have you ever been disciplined by the Lord Jesus? Well, I was that morning. I had been sitting thinking of all things that I didn't want to endure instead of thanking my Jesus for all the things that I had been given. As soon as I read the Scripture, I understood why he wanted me to read it. I had gotten in trouble for worrying about the future. I knew better. I was well aware that there should be no place for fretting, anxiousness, or worrying within the course of my day. What was I to say? I was guilty as charged.

"Lord Jesus, I am sorry. I know you hold the future within your hands. I trust you completely in whatever path you choose for Jon, Danny, Jonna, and me. Forgive me for dwelling on the tomorrows. I thank you for my todays." As my mother-in-law would say, "Boy, howdy!" I felt about two inches tall, yet thankful that Jesus took the time to correct me. Now, I really did have to finish getting myself ready for school. Jonna's alarm was set to go off momentarily, and I needed to be finished so I could start breakfast. That morning had turned out to be eventful. I hadn't been expecting anything as it had been.

Jonna's alarm signaled her wake-up time. Routinely, she was awake the instant her ears heard the clock telling her it was time to get out of bed. This morning was no different. I was already in the kitchen banging around the pans to fix breakfast when I heard the bathroom door shutting. Bacon was frying and eggs were cooking when my little sleepyhead walked into the kitchen to get juice from the fridge. After retrieving her glass of juice, Jonna paddled into the bedroom to get ready for her drive to school. It wasn't long until my sleepy-eyed baby girl returned into the kitchen dressed, bright-eyed, and ready to scarf down breakfast before driving to school.

"Gotta go, Momma! See ya at school! Love ya!" she popped up from the barstool and said. As I picked up the breakfast dishes, I could see the sun's reflection on the truck. I watched the brilliant flashes of red grow dim as her truck finished its trek down the little country road in front of our house. "Lord Jesus, let your angels drive with her," I said as I watched the truck travel over the hill and out of sight. The dishes were hurriedly washed and put away, the cats were fed, and my morning chores were completed. I grabbed my purse and headed for my car.

The inside of the car was quiet during the morning commute. As a rule, I turned on the Christian radio station and sang songs of praise while I drove. However, that morning I didn't want music to interfere with my meditation of the Scripture the Holy Spirit had conveyed to me that morning. "Sufficient today is the evil thereof" replayed itself over and over in my mind. Of course, as those words kept coming to me, I was reminded that there was a great tribulation still coming, but *not to worry* (emphasis belonged to the Lord).

After hearing those words, I felt my spiritual strength level go from 99 percent to 100 percent. I would never forget how I felt each time the Holy Spirit filled my spiritual strength tank a little fuller. Each time I received an appointed amount of strength, I also received a proportional amount of peace, his peace. Awesome? To say the least, it was an awesome feeling. For the past six months, I would feel his presence and receive his gifts of strength and peace in what I thought to be abnormal amounts. This was the reason that I absolutely knew that something was going to happen in my life—something really, really difficult. My Jesus knew exactly what it would take for me to endure whatever it was that was going to come my way.

I had no doubt that he would take care of me. I had no doubt that he wouldn't carry me through it. I just had doubts as to what was coming, and that particular Monday morning, as I heard his voice once again; I began to really wonder what was knocking on my door in a "big" way. In fact, for the first time, I openly asked Jesus to tell me. I questioned, I asked, and I (kind of) pleaded. My words were in vain, however. They were replaced only by a dreadful silence within the interior of my little car. The silence was my answer. In other words, I knew through the silence that he was not going to tell me. I knew that "sufficient unto this day is the evil thereof," and I understood that the future was not mine to know. I didn't like the feeling that was within my spirit amidst the fog of silence. I dwelt there in the fog until I realized that I had passed the turn to school. In reality, I had nearly driven ten miles past the turn. As a result, my reality immediately took a turn from spiritual to physical when I pulled onto a country road that directed my car back towards its intended arrival point. Even with every attempt to make it to my classroom before the last bell without getting a speeding ticket, my heart pondered on the spiritual encounter that was held within my car that morning.

Chapter Forty

Out of Sight

AFTER DRIVING THE EXTRA TWENTY miles this morning on my commute, I pulled into the school's parking lot and hurried to my classroom. One of the advantages of being a music teacher was that I had no attendance to check, lunches to count, or early-morning rituals to take care of. Therefore, my first class of the morning didn't actually show up until the third grade teacher walked them from the elementary side of the school to the music room, which was located in the high school section. So, in reality I was only a few minutes late, according to the clock on the wall. I still had plenty of time to get organized for third-grade music.

This Monday was typical of Mondays. The first day of the school week is spent reviewing, listening to both heartwarming and earth-shattering stories of how the past weekend was spent, and somehow maintaining some kind of curricular activities. I didn't hear from Jonna that morning. The cliché "out of sight, out of mind" held true. I actually didn't realize that she hadn't peeked into the music room door until the lunch bell rang at 11:20. Then, I wondered what had kept her from barging into my room to say "Hi, Momma!" I wasn't worried, though. Even though it was rare that she didn't show her smiling face two or three times a day, there had been days that she neglected to pop in until after school. As I said, I wasn't concerned because I was off to the cafeteria. It was salad time, and I knew I would see her there.

Sure enough, no sooner than I reached the cafeteria door, I heard laughter coming from the back corner of the cafeteria. I knew the guilty parties of the uncontrolled giggling without having to walk through the door. I don't know what had kicked off the epidemic of laughter, but it was definitely contagious. As I looked around, it seemed that almost everyone, student, teacher and staff, had a smile on their face. Yep! Those were my girls (I say "girls" because Jonna wasn't the only one responsible for the smiles that day; there were about four others sitting at the table as well).

With my salad in hand, I hurried over to the lunch table where they sat. "You know if you were in grade school, you wouldn't be allowed to make so much noise," I said. I was telling the truth about the noise level during grade school lunch, but I was being sarcastic with these young women. The reply I received was, "Oh! We are so sorry. We will try to be quieter." With a smile, I said, "Don't you dare. You are making everyone smile, too!" With that being said, I took my salad to the teachers' table totally content.

Only the Lord Jesus really understood how wonderful my days were because I shared them with my daughter. No other words were exchanged between us that day . . . none were needed. I had seen the beautiful joy of the Lord penetrating through her spirit, as well as the other girls who were sitting with Jonna. Sometimes, words simply don't do justice to the circumstance. The glory of the Lord Jesus was hovering over that lunch table that day, and there were simply no other words that needed to be spoken. I relished in the overwhelming discernment I was feeling, finished my lunch, and floated back to my classroom to prepare for my afternoon classes. "Thank you, Lord Jesus! Just . . . thank you," were the only words that my heart was speaking.

Monday afternoon came and went. As soon as the last bell sounded, I gathered up some change and walked down the hallway to get a pop out of the machine. This activity took patience at the end of the day because baseball players, softball players, teachers, and any student who was staying after school for whatever reason darted to the vending machines at the 2:15 bell. I waited in line listening to different students recall their day to friends. I remembered Jonna had softball practice instead of work, and I kept my eyes out for her. Finally, I saw her coming down the hallway with a few of the other players from the softball team. They had already changed into practice attire and were coming to the vending machines before practice started.

"How was your day?" I asked Jonna. "Good, Momma. How was yours?" she replied.

After acknowledging her question, I realized it was my turn to get something to quench my thirst. I heard my change jangle into the machine and the thud of a can of pop hit the bottom of the receiving bin.

Quickly, I retrieved it and walked toward my baby girl. Upon hearing her say that she was coming straight home from practice, I hugged her and walked back to my room to grade research papers from my high school music appreciation class. As I sat down to read papers, I hoped I would be in the right frame of mind to complete the task at hand. I had read several music research papers through the years and was never surprised at what some of them would say. Whether it be good, bad, or ugly, no topic or word was ever beyond belief.

After reading just a few, I paused and wondered how long Jonna's practice would be that afternoon. For an instant, I thought I would just finish up and go watch practice for a while. But upon second thought, I decided to drive on home and fix a nice dinner for my hubby and my baby.

Chapter Forty-One

Prom

THE NEXT MORNING, JONNA and I were up early. I don't know why, but we both were awake before either of our alarms signaled our wake-up calls. I was thankful, though. It always heralded the start of a wonderful day when we had a few minutes to chill and talk in the mornings. Jonna had bounced out of her bed this morning more chipper than usual. I knew the reason without even asking. Today at school started prom decorations and planning. It was always a fun time of year for the high-school juniors and seniors. In other words, it seemed that the upper two classes of high school students didn't have much academic responsibility starting today. Jonna was all set for her senior prom.

She had gone dress shopping and found the perfect dress. I think her daddy would have liked it to have had a little more material, but it was beautiful, and she was beautiful in it. I never had to worry about Jonna's taste in clothing because she held tightly to 1 Timothy 2:9:"Women should adorn themselves in modest apparel." The flower for her date had been ordered, and everything was ready except for manicures, pedicures, and hair. But, those would be taken care of Friday night and Saturday.

Prom wasn't the only reason Jonna was elated that morning. To-night was the Honors Dinner she had been asked to attend. This dinner was held annually to pay tribute to those students of southern Illinois who had been nominated by school administration based on character, virtue, and academic achievement. I knew I was filled with partiality, but in my opinion, this young woman deserved the honor. Jonna had proven that she was instilled with all the necessary characteristics.

But, of course, my daughter was indwelled by the Holy Spirit, and reflected the fruits of the Spirit with humility and love. She understood that the fruits of the Spirit were the ingredients needed to be an effective witness for the Lord Jesus, and she willingly allowed the Holy Spirit to let his light shine through her. In fact, "virtue" by Biblical definition is the "fruit of the Holy Spirit." Jonna was determined to fulfill the role which the Lord had prepared her for—a life spent for him. As a result, she often meditated on these words:

> But the fruit of the Spirit is love, joy, peace, longsuffering [patience], gentleness [kindness], goodness, faith, meekness, temperance [self-control] . . .
>
> Galatians 5:22–23

Jonna prayed that the world would be able to see Jesus through her, and because she heeded the Holy Spirit, his character combined with Jonna's individual desire to love life made my daughter the young woman she was. The invitation to this event gave her an uplifting encouragement to continue on through her college years not changing anything. But then, Jonna couldn't change unless the Lord prompted it. My angel was the sole property of her Lord Jesus! I knew it, respected it, and marveled at it. I often thought that if I could have just half of the relationship with Jesus that my daughter had, I would be okay.

Yes, that morning I absolutely knew that this day was only the beginning of a fun week for my baby. I watched her sitting at the table and eating breakfast this morning and saw a vision of a little, bouncy, dark-haired toddler scarfing down her cereal because she just *had* to attend to other matters and decisions of the day. As I saw that precious memory fade into the beautiful woman sitting and eating her cereal, a tear or two slid down my cheeks. Where did my baby go? Wasn't it only yesterday she was eating cereal with her Care Bear spoon and drinking juice from her sippy cup? Yes, I missed those days, but the joy of seeing her grow into the young woman now sitting in front of me was indescribable. I never realized how I would long for the days of bedtime stories and tucking my angel in bed with her favorite of all-favorite friends, Piggy Doll. I just didn't realize . . .

Chapter Forty-Two

Heartbreak

THE DAY PROGRESSED AS normally as possible. My daily schedule as a music teacher gave way to no major problems, inconveniences, or disruptions. Each class that day was dedicated to rehearsals for the upcoming spring concert. As concert time was rapidly approaching, there was still very much rehearsing that needed to be done. As usual, the junior high choir was more than performance ready, and because of their readiness, their class time was the only relaxing rehearsal that was engaged that day.

When the lunch bell rang, I managed to squirm between high school students who seemed in no hurry to go to lunch. As I wiggled in and out of student groups which had congregated to discuss prom, I noticed that I didn't see Jonna amidst the crowd. As soon as I comprehended the idea that she wasn't in the hallway, I had already entered the grade-school annex which held the cafeteria. Sure enough, there she sat at the favorite lunch table of her circle of friends. Something was very out of sync, though. She was eating her lunch quietly and alone.

Immediately, my spirit was aware there was a problem, and I headed quickly over to the lonely table which was entertained only by my baby. My first response was to reach out and tug on her hair, which was dangled behind her head in ponytail style. But no sooner than I started to reach for it, she turned around. "Momma, this day sucks!" were the first words out of her mouth. Upon hearing these disconnected words, I sat down beside her and asked her what was going on.

"It just sucks! I am tired and stressed out. I just want to go home, pull the covers up over me and sleep. Nothing has gone right this morning. The first person I saw in the hallway was the only person I cared about seeing. Guess what he did? Nothing! He just sort of smiled, turned away, and walked off down the hall. I don't get it. I thought we were best friends."

I didn't know what to say. I realized her best friend was ignoring her, and I honestly knew how she felt. I mean, we have all been there, right? But it seemed to hurt my heart way more because it was my baby hurting instead of me. What was I to say? I thought that she had sorted her way through this heartbreak. Now, after a few months, I realized that this was the boy she loved. This was the love of her life and had been since her freshman year. The problem was that she assumed he felt the same way, but upon discovering that he didn't, my little girl's heart, spirit, and soul were crushed.

"Jonna," I said, "Come on and try to cheer up. Try thinking about prom and how much fun you will have. Try thinking about the boy you are dating now. I know you care for him, and I truly believe that he cares for you. Once you graduate here and start college, there will be so many to choose from that you won't believe it. College boys are completely different. You will meet boys from all over southern Illinois. The only problem you will have is making sure that the Lord wants you to go out with them. Who knows?"

"Momma, it's not just that. You remember when I told you that I didn't fit here and that I wanted to go home? *That's* what is wrong. I don't, and I *do*! I love being with my friends, and I am looking forward to prom. I love playing ball, and I can't wait to sign the contract for college ball Friday morning, but my spirit, deep down, is uneasy. I guess I am just tired."

Now what? I asked myself. The only logical answer to those words came out of this momma's mouth without hesitation. "Why don't you go sign out and go home. You can crawl up in bed, turn TV on, and rest. I will tell Coach that you weren't feeling well and won't be at the game today. You don't have to go to Carbondale to the dinner tonight. Just stay home, rest, and sleep." I earnestly prayed that she would take my advice, but she didn't.

"No, Momma. I gotta play in the game, and I have already made plans to drive to the dinner with the other girls who are going. I can't just think of myself. I will be okay. I just got down for a little while. I am glad that you came over, though. It helped to talk. You are the only one I can talk to about this without upsetting someone. Thank you."

I heard her words, but I didn't believe them. I could feel her heartache. "Lord Jesus! You have to help my baby. You need to do something to restore this relationship because the silence between them is tearing her apart. If the truth is known, I would guess that he's quite upset, too. Please work this out. I can't stand to see her like this. She has so much to look forward to, and right now, she can't see the forest for the trees. Now, I thank you for listening to ME. I know you will help her sort through this. I know you will." These were the words that came pouring out of my heart to Jesus, and I believed every one of them. I had no doubt that he would help her deal with this until this relationship could be resolved.

After all, teenage years are for experiencing situations and learning from them. At least that's what I tried to comfort myself with. The only obstacle to that theory was both people involved were young adults now. Their "best-friend" relationship had always come first because they truly were best friends. I could read the signs, and I totally understood something that they didn't. First love, true love, only love? Only Jesus knew for sure how long love would stick around, but for now all I knew was that they loved each other and had for a long time. But I also realized that *they* had to work it out for themselves. No sir, I was not going to be the go-between.

Well, as I gave Jonna a hug and walked to the salad bar to fix my lunch, I heard familiar giggling echo from the doorway. "Good! Here come the rest of the lunch room crew. Now, she won't be by herself," I said. Whether I said it to the Lord, myself, or simply thought it, I don't remember. But a sigh of relief came as I saw her smile at the group.

I was sincerely thankful for the timing of Jonna's friends' entrance to the lunchroom. It had given us time to talk and had given me the blessing of watching the smiles of the kids I had learned to love and the daughter whom I loved more than life itself. I felt a familiar peace return to my spirit, and I was reminded that the Lord Jesus was with me and that the Holy Spirit was within me. "Thank you, Lord Jesus. Thank you, Holy Spirit. Thank you for loving me so much."

As soon as I felt the peace of Jesus and his warmth travel through my body, I decided to take the rest of my lunch back to the classroom. With a smile, I acknowledged the truth that Jonna was in good hands at this moment, and I could desperately use some quiet time behind the door of my room. So off I went, lunch in hand, to the confines of my room. I did something that day that I didn't usually do.

I locked the door to make sure the remainder of my lunch hour was quiet. I needed some "me time." However, amidst the peace of my Jesus, my spirit was unsettled. I didn't know why. I knew better than to talk to

Jesus about the culprit of this feeling. I imagined it had something to do with a "great tribulation" which was still in the future. But, through experience, I learned that the One who holds my future wouldn't give up that information. So, without asking, I decided to just eat my lunch and think about the upcoming concert.

Chapter Forty-Three

His Throne

THE REMAINDER OF THE afternoon passed quickly. As usual, Jonna stuck her head through the door as she left school. She was dressed in her softball uniform as number 7 for the important game that afternoon.

By the way, I believe I failed to mention that the number seven on her jersey was picked by my baby. If you are not aware of the significance of this number, please let me enlighten you. The number seven throughout Scripture signified our Father God's perfect number. There are lots of examples in the Bible where our God used this number. Perhaps the most noted one is that the Creation took seven days; well, six days and the Sabbath. However, the one that always comes to my mind concerns the Holy Spirit.

> And the spirit of the Lord shall rest upon him, the spirit of wisdom and understanding, the spirit of counsel and might, the spirit of knowledge and the fear (respect) of the Lord.
>
> Isaiah 11:2
>
> John to the seven churches which are in Asia: Grace be unto you, and peace, from him which is, which was, and which is to come; and from the seven Spirits which are before his throne.
>
> Revelation 1:4

The seven Spirits of the Holy Spirit mentioned in Revelation were the seven-fold ministries of the Holy Spirit. In other words, the Holy Spirit in his fullness!

Jonna and the Lord, as I have said, were so close. By this time in her life, she had given evidence of every gift of the Spirit mentioned in Scripture.

- Word of Wisdom—not the everyday wisdom that each of us would like to proclaim that we have, but the wisdom that was spoken through the utterance of the Holy Spirit that applied to a revelation of God's word or the Spirit's wisdom for a specific situation or problem.

- Word of Knowledge—words inspired by the Holy Spirit that showed knowledge about people, circumstances, or Biblical truth

- Gift of Faith—not the saving faith, but the kind of faith that allowed a Christian to believe God for the extraordinary and miraculous.

- Gifts of Healing—the gift that was given to restore physical health by divine means

- Miracles—deeds of supernatural power which altered the course of things in the physical world

- Prophecy—a gift that allowed a believer to bring a word or message directly from God, through the voice of the Spirit, to the church or individuals

- Discernment of Spirits—a special ability given by the Spirit to be able to distinguish between spiritual good and evil, truth and lie

- Tongues—a supernatural manifestation of the Spirit which allowed a spirit of man and the Spirit of God to entwine so that the believer communicates directly to God

- Interpretation of Tongues—the supernatural ability given by the Holy Spirit to understand a message given in tongues.

Yes, that was my little girl. Never would I ever have dreamed that early morning on January 29, 1983, that the precious little girl that I held would be so strong in the power and might of our Lord Jesus. Yes, I knew from the beginning of her young life that she would be used by God, but to this extent, never in my wildest dreams.

However improbable or impossible one may think, that was who my little girl had become. Jonna was definitely "full" of the Holy Spirit; yet, she had the ability to not think more highly of herself than she should. She was nothing more than a humble servant of the Lord Jesus. Humility walked with her daily. She never proclaimed to do anything without giving all the glory to her Jesus. She never did anything without directly communicating with him for direction. She didn't have any pride within her; however, she did portray a confidence in her Lord Jesus and all the things that he did through her. It was this confidence in him that led her to ask that the number 7 be placed on her softball jersey. This number was her testimony and witness during each and every game when she wore it.

So that afternoon was no different than any other game day except for one thing: Jonna's arms were carrying not only her catcher's gear for the game, but clinging on to hangers with clothes for the honors dinner that night. She had decided to leave from the game and drive directly to Southern Illinois University, where the dinner was to be held. Of course, a girl had to have her makeup, hair rollers, blow dryer, dress clothes, etc.

We had discussed my attendance at the dinner for a couple of days, and had come to a mutual agreement that it wasn't necessary. Yes, I would have liked to be there. Yes, I knew that I should have gone the minute I saw the red truck leave the school parking lot. Yes, I knew that Jonna wanted me to go, but Jonna being Jonna understood that I was tired. "Momma, you should go home, put your feet up, and rest," she told me. "I will see you when I get home. It's okay." So I went home after school and regretted every minute that I wasn't there with my baby.

Later that night, I heard the truck pull into the gravel driveway on Spring Valley Road. I was so very thankful that she had gotten home safely, because without a doubt she was the one who was worn to a frazzle. As I heard the truck door slam, I hurried to the porch door to give her a big hug.

"Jonna, I am so sorry I didn't go with you. I should have been there. I should have been with you tonight," were the first words out of this momma's mouth. I will never forget the expression on her face as she said, "It's okay. It was no big deal. The dinner was nice, but I would have rather been at home. You know the old saying, 'There's no place like home.' I love you, but I am going to bed now. See ya in the morning."

I knew that she was trying to make me feel better about not going to the dinner, but somehow within my spirit, I felt guilty. Looking back, I realized that it wasn't necessarily all guilt that I felt. I understood completely that my spirit was torn. After helping Jonna bring the remainder of her things into the house, I sat down in my favorite rocking chair hoping to figure out the emotion that was encompassing my spirit. If it wasn't guilt, what was it?

Jonna did exactly what she had intended. Within minutes, she was snuggled up within the confines of covers on her bed, sound asleep. Confident that my baby was safe and secure within the walls of home, I took a deep breath and began talking to my Jesus. The only thing I knew to do when I don't know what to say was let the Holy Spirit do the talking for me. I depended on one of the gifts of the Spirit—my ability to pray in tongues. I didn't know what was wrong within my spirit nor did I begin to know what to say to my Jesus.

So, for the next little while, Jesus and I talked it over with the help of the Holy Spirit, who was definitely telling the Lord what my heart didn't know what to say. The three of us sat there until I realized a peace had overwhelmed my spirit and sleep was overtaking my eyes. As I struggled to keep my eyelids open, I carved a path directly to the bedroom, moved Casper across the foot of the bed, manipulated Mozart off of my pillow, snuggled up to my hubby, and slept.

Chapter Forty-Four

The Eye of the Storm

Fear not that the whirlwind shall carry thee hence,
Nor wait for its onslaught in breathless suspense,
Nor shrink from the whips of the terrible hail,
But pass through the edge to the heart of the tale,
For there is a shelter, sun lighted and warm,
And Faith sees her God through the eye of the storm.

The passionate tempest with rush and wild roar
And threatenings of evil may beat on the shore,
The waves may be mountains, the fields battle plains,
And the earth be immersed in a deluge of rains,
Yet, the soul, stayed on God, may sing bravely its psalm,
For the heart of the storm is the center of calm.

Let hope be not quenched in the blackness of night,
Though the cyclone awhile may have blotted the light,
For behind the great darkness the stars ever shine,
And the light of God's heavens, his love shall make thine.
Let no gloom dim thine eyes, but uplift them on high
To the face of thy God and the blue of his sky.

The storm is thy shelter from danger and sin,
And God himself takes you for safety within;
The tempest with him passeth into deep calm,
And the roar of the winds is the sound of a psalm.
Be glad and serene when the tempest clouds form;
God smiles on his child in the eye of the storm.

—Unknown

Chapter Forty-Five

Honors Day

THURSDAY, MAY 3, 2001, had begun as a beautifully sunny spring day. As the alarm beside my bed chimed out its news that it was time to get out of my warm cocoon of covers, the first thing I noticed was how brightly the sun was peeping in through the blinds that covered the eastern windows of the bedroom. Jon had already left for work. Mozart had evidently decided to take possession of Jon's pillow as my long-haired bed companion was sleeping soundly within the indentations of his soft bed. As I lay there trying to talk myself into pushing the covers back, I heard the birds chirp their morning songs of spring. However cheerfully the morning displayed her beauty, I had no idea that the events of this day would forever be etched into the portals of my soul and spirit.

Finally, after releasing a huge sigh, I looked over at Mozart and said, "Okay, Mozart. Rise and shine." Of course, the only response I received from him was nothing. It wasn't until I started straightening the covers that he raised his head, meowed, and without any urgency managed to jump down so I could finish the task of making the bed. As soon as the final pillow was covered with the bedspread, I ventured into the kitchen for morning coffee.

It was then that I was aware of Jonna's alarm singing its wake-up song. Evidently, she wasn't too interested in rising and shining that morning, either. The alarm rang, rang, and rang some more until it evolved to complete silence. She had reached over, touched the snooze button, and drifted back to sleep. "I will let her sleep a few more minutes," I thought. "Then if she doesn't get up, I will go wake her up." But I didn't have to. As soon as the snooze time was up, the alarm broke the silence in her bedroom once more. This time, though, I heard the alarm stop and the sound of her bedroom door being pushed over the carpet.

In just a few minutes, my sleepy-eyed angel was walking into the kitchen to eat breakfast. We talked about the day's schedule, which included High School Honors Day at school and a softball game at 4:00. No sooner than she was finished eating, than she popped up from the bar stool and said, "Momma, I don't think I am going to stay for Honors Day today. Would you care to get whatever awards I get for me?"

"Don't you want to be there to get your own? What are you going to do?" I asked.

"I think I will leave school after lunch and drive to my friend's house and take a nap before my game," was her answer. I knew she was tired so I agreed. With that being decided on, the rest of the morning at Spring Valley Road was right on schedule. As I was getting ready, I heard, "Momma, come here a minute," echoing down the hallway. Jonna said she had been thinking and had decided that after her game she was going to go to her boyfriend's band rehearsal.

"Jonna, you are tired. You need to come on home and get some rest. If you go to the rehearsal, you will be completely worn out."

"No, I won't. I will be fine. I want to hear the rehearsal and see him," she stated. I knew that it wasn't going to do any good if I argued with her. I knew that she had her mind made up, but I thought I would give it one last try. "Jonna, I really think you better come on home. He will understand. Besides, you're gonna see him this weekend." Well, those words went in one ear and out the other as she matter-of-factly informed me that she was going to the rehearsal. "Okay," I said, "but just for the record, Momma thinks it's a bad idea."

After the conversation was over, I finished getting ready for work. As a rule, Jonna was the first one out of the door in the mornings, but this morning I was done first. Before I left, however, I walked toward her bedroom and said, "Bye, sweetheart. I will see ya at school."

"Okay. Bye," were the only words she said. I remember thinking how grumpy she was acting and said, "Lord Jesus, she's tired. Please let your angels drive with her to school." After my morning request, I started the car, pulled out of the driveway, and headed for work.

The morning went as planned—concert rehearsals for each class period. Before I knew it, the lunch bell sounded. As I watched the junior high choir filing out of the music room door, there was no need to rush to the cafeteria for lunch. Because of the high school awards program that afternoon, the rest of my classes for the day were cancelled. I relished the idea of eating my lunch with no deadline, so I took my time.

I decided to straighten up the room a little and grade some papers before eating. When those tasks were completed, I headed toward the cafeteria to have my daily salad. I realized that I had taken longer than I thought when I approached the lunchroom's door and noticed that Jonna and her friends had already eaten and left. "Oh, well," I thought to myself, "I will see her at the game later on." I wasn't concerned that she wasn't there. I thought she might have gone ahead and left so she could take a nap. As I ate, the rest of the high school kids eventually left the cafeteria, which gave way to complete quiet. "What a nice way to eat lunch," I thought, "This doesn't happen very often." However, just as I was finishing, the bell rang and the sound of grade-school students entering the cafeteria and trying their best to speak in "inside voices" quickly overtook the silence.

The minutes passed quickly, and before I could finish grading the stack of music appreciation papers, it was time to go to the gym. While sitting in the teacher's section and talking to some of the other high school teachers, I wasn't paying any attention to the high school students as they made their way onto the bleachers in the gym. I remembered that Jonna said she wasn't going to be there, and that I needed to make note of any awards she was to receive. Because I didn't want to neglect to pick up any awards from the giving teacher, I decided to write them down so I wouldn't overlook any.

However, after just a few minutes, Jonna's name was announced for her first achievement. Before I could write the award down, however, I noticed that she was headed to the podium to receive the award. I asked myself, "Wonder why she went ahead and stayed?" I was happy to see her there, but I was a little confused. I knew that she really wanted to get some rest before the softball game that afternoon. I noticed something that maybe only I would notice, however. I detected a look of sadness in her face. I was aware that she had been a little short with me that morning, but I didn't believe that there was any reason except she was physically tired.

The look on her face disturbed me, though. I could read through her expressions of forced smiles and appreciation for the honors she received. It was as though my spirit was crying out and sharing her sorrow. Even though I had no idea the culprit behind the sadness, I felt ill-at-ease and uncertain.

Finally, the program was over and all awards had been received. The clock on the gym wall showed that there was only about forty-five minutes until the end of the school day, and because of that time, our principal instructed everyone to go to their last-period classes. This, for me, would be high school choir. The thought occurred to me, "Do we rehearse or just chill?" I didn't dwell very long upon this question, however, as I made the executive decision to relax. I knew from experience that by the time all the students managed to stop visiting and find their way to the music room, there would only be a few minutes until the final bell rang.

As the high school halls were full of students who were in no hurry to go to class, it took me longer than usual to walk to the music room. I didn't mind though, because I was trying to see if I could find Jonna in the midst of the bustle. But upon reaching my appointed destination, I realized that she was nowehere to be found, so I was satisfied that she had finally left school and gone to her friend's house to rest. I did, however, look out of the back door window to see if her truck was still in the parking lot. The spot where she had parked that morning was empty, so there was nothing more to do except unlock my classroom door and wait for the choir kids to come inside. Because I had been their teacher since many of the choir members were small, I was familiar with the sound of their individual voices, giggles, and laughs, which enabled me to know exactly which students were walking towards the classroom.

Just as I had predicted, by the time they were all accounted for, the final forty-five minutes of the school day were now down to twenty-five minutes. To my amazement, some of the girls had asked to sing whatever they wanted instead of rehearsing for the concert. This sounded like a great idea to me since there was only time enough to sing a few songs anyway. Some of the girls were in the process of deciding on which songs they would like to sing when I heard a knock at the music room door. As I started toward the door to open it, I realized it was already open. Standing in the doorway was an employee of the school.

I knew in my heart something was wrong. I just knew.

Chapter Forty-Six

Tribulation Day

As I CONTINUED WALKING toward her, she said, "Mrs. Shackleford, there has been an accident." I remember saying, "What happened?" and she proceeded to inform me that Jonna had been in an accident just down the road from school. I didn't need to hear anymore, and as I turned to get my purse, I told her, "I'm going!" I didn't even think about supervision for the class, I didn't consider anything except getting to my baby.

As soon as I was ready to pull onto the road beside the school, I was suddenly interrupted by the sound of an approaching ambulance. My heart sank, but as I sat in the car waiting for the ambulance to pass, I was determined that I knew what I would find. I was absolutely positive that as soon as I approached the accident site, I would see Jonna standing on the side of the road crying because she was scared and the truck was wrecked. As quickly as the speeding ambulance came within my sight, it vanished. My little red car pulled out onto the road as my spirit was praying, "Lord Jesus, please let her be okay. Please let her be okay!"

The site was only about three miles down the road from school. I expected to see a few people standing around her, comforting my baby, and calming her. It's extremely overwhelming how many thoughts a mind can think in the matter of a couple of minutes. What was a short drive, a drive that I had taken many, many times, seemed like an eternity that day. I actually don't even remember the drive itself. I wasn't prepared for the scene at the end of it. What I had expected to find was magnified to an extent that I couldn't begin to comprehend it.

Cars and people everywhere. The country road was so congested that I couldn't even drive to where my baby was. Cars were pulled off the road and parked in the grass on both sides of that little country highway.

166

In front of me was a policeman who was signaling for me to turn down the other road. I just stopped! I just couldn't take the time to explain to him that my daughter was up that road and I needed to get through. I didn't even think about telling him. I just stopped the car, opened the door, and got out. I remember hearing the patrolman yelling, "Lady, you can't leave your car there. Hey! Hey!"

I started walking toward the intended spot. As I walked, I realized that I wasn't going to see Jonna standing on the side of the road. My spirit knew differently. Because of that, I ran. I just ran. I ran until I was able to see. It was my complete intention to keep going until I reached the truck that my baby was nestled in. All I knew was I had to get to her—to touch her—to reassure her that I was there with her. However, good intentions don't always play out.

Another county policeman grabbed me and informed me that I couldn't go down there. "I *am* going! That's my baby. That's my little girl." I remember his kind voice trying to explain to me that the rescue vehicle was on its way, and I needed to stay back until they got her out. Upon hearing his words, I dropped to my knees there in the middle of the road. All I knew to do was cry out to my Jesus. I couldn't tell you who the people were that were congregated around that spot, and I surely had no idea how many were there. Miles of people, tons of people, hundreds of people? I didn't have a clue, and I didn't care. I fell to my knees and prayed. How was I supposed to pray, Lord Jesus? What am I supposed to say? All I knew to say was, "Please let her be *okay.*" Over and over again, those were the only words I could say. In just a matter of moments, the Holy Spirit came to my aide, and I began to pray in the Spirit.

> Likewise the Spirit also helpeth our infirmities: for we know not what we should pray for as we ought: but the Spirit itself maketh intercession for us with groanings which cannot be uttered.

Romans 8:26

That afternoon, the Holy Spirit prayed to my Jesus for me. It was the Holy Spirit, the Comforter whom Jesus sent to me, who knew that I couldn't manage to speak the things that I longed to say to my Jesus. It was the Third Person of the Trinity coming to my rescue. Because he lived within my heart, he, alone, knew my suffering and pain that afternoon. As a result of understanding the "groaning" that was within me, he interceded and prayed for me. He uttered the words that I couldn't find in me to speak that afternoon.

It didn't matter that countless others no doubt heard my prayers through the language of the Holy Spirit. It didn't even cross my mind that anyone was even around me. All I comprehended was that my baby was in that truck, they wouldn't let me get to her, and that I needed my Lord Jesus. I had withdrawn into a spiritual realm that included my Jesus, the Holy Spirit, and me. I had no idea how much time passed until my prayers were interrupted when I felt a touch upon my back. I turned my head to see Jonna's blue Bible being handed to me by the boy who was to escort her to prom that weekend.

An all-too-surreal situation because the young man and his mother, who was a teacher at the school and coworker/dear friend to me were traveling down the same highway, right behind Jonna. Of course, they witnessed the accident and were on the scene as soon as it occurred. I have prayed throughout these past years many, *many* times for the two of them. Both cared deeply for my little girl. Both saw more than I saw on that road. I have nightmares from time to time still. Do they? I have often asked. I prayerfully have requested that my Lord protect them from the scars of May 3, 2001, and that he bless them abundantly for being there for me that sunny yet dark afternoon. As I reached out to take the Bible from his hand, he explained that he had gotten it from her truck. I thanked him, and proceeded with my prayers.

Once again, I had shut out the confusion around me. Once again my vocal prayers were said amidst the crowd of teachers, students, parents, and bystanders whom had gathered as soon as the final bell at school rang. Once again my prayer language filled the air, traveled through the atmosphere, and kept going until it reached the throne of Jesus. Did I understand what was being said during my prayers? No, I didn't. Nor did I take the time for the Holy Spirit to give me any interpretation. The language of the angels just kept flooding out of my mouth.

Suddenly, my ears picked up on the sound of another siren approaching. It was the emergency rescue unit. I gathered my senses enough to realize that they were there to get my baby out of the truck that she was pinned into. Upon the unit's arrival, the voice of the policeman standing nearby rang in my ears: "Ma'am, let's get you out of this confusion. Come sit in the squad car until your daughter is freed. Please, Ma'am." The officer helped me up from the ground and gently led me to the police car. It was then that the kind, compassionate officer informed me what had happened. I solemnly sat in the driver's seat of that squad car and as tears rolled down my cheeks onto the black leather seat covers, I shut my eyes tightly and just listened.

Evidently, as Jonna was on her way to her friend's house to relax and try to sleep awhile before her softball game that afternoon, she approached a hilltop on the road. On the opposite side of the highway coming toward her was a farm tractor with corn planters attached. Jonna had evidently seen the tractor on the road's hilltop. What was blocked from her vision, however, were the descended corn planters. Instead of being upward in a traveling position, the tractor driver had left them down. As a result, her side of the roadway was blocked due to the extended arms of the tractor.

She didn't—or couldn't—see the arm of the planter until it topped the hill. By then, it was too late! No skid marks, no tire marks, no jet-black anything, signaling that she hadn't tried to stop or even slow down. Because of the clear, unmarked pavement, the officer said she had hit the tractor's extended limb head-on with no unforeseen knowledge that she needed to slow her little red truck down to prevent an accident.

In case you missed it amidst my rambling, the hilltop of the road was blocking Jonna's vision; she could not see over the top of this hill. She had no idea that the coming tractor's arms were in her direct path. She couldn't see what shouldn't have been there. She didn't know what was coming nor what hit her. In fact, because she was unconscious, the first responders and the doctors said she never knew anything. No pain, no confusion, no fear—nothing. Or, at least if she did, her mental status was only on alert for a matter of a few seconds.

After listening intently to the policeman's summary of the occurrence, I just sat there praying without ceasing. Once again, the Spirit took over. One more time, I depended upon him to pray for me. From the driver's seat of the squad car, I could only see people and faces. However, among the crowd, I noticed the solitary tractor which was responsible for the deeply-inflicted wounds my baby had sustained. I wondered where the tractor's driver was, who he was, and if he was critically injured as well, but that's as far as the notion went, because I found myself tossed back deeply into my prayer world.

It seemed as though only a few seconds had passed until another police officer approached the vehicle in which I had been placed and informed me that they had gotten Jonna out of the truck. He said they were loading her into the ambulance to take her to the emergency room at the closest hospital. With that information, I got out of the car, and headed toward the ambulance. However, by the time I got to the emergency vehicle, they were getting ready to shut the door and take off. "Wait!" I yelled, "Please wait! I'm her momma. I am going with you."

As if no one heard my plea, the door was shut and the siren raged. I ran to the last member of the crew before she entered the unit. "Please let me go. That's my daughter," I cried out. It didn't matter how much I begged, she said I couldn't go. I turned to see my coworker, whose son had handed me Jonna's Bible earlier. "Where are your keys? I will drive you," were the words I heard her speak. To this day, I don't remember if my keys were in my purse, my pants pocket, or the ignition of my car. I just knew that she drove me behind the screaming sirens of the ambulance. Once again, while she drove, I prayed. I want to take this opportunity to make sure that it is understood how very much I appreciated her presence and her help that day. She will never know how thankful I was for her.

During the course of the next hour, there were far too many events to mention on the pages of this book. I remember seeing faces of students, teachers, and friends. Doctors were coming and going. Nurses were entering the waiting room and then leaving. My vocal prayers had subsided because I was filling out paperwork for medical insurance, answering questions on Jonna's medical history, and talking to others. During a brief interlude from medical inquiries, I asked for a telephone so I could call Jonna's brother. As soon as I had hung up the phone, a doctor approached and asked me to come with him.

As we walked, he proceeded to explain to me the extent of Jonna's injuries. "We are going to life-flight her to a trauma center in St. Louis," he said, "but don't worry. She's young, healthy, and I hear that she's an athlete. She will recover." The words "she will recover" were the only words I clung to. I heard the doctor say them, but why wasn't I feeling them? As he led me into the E.R. cubicle where my little girl was, he explained to me that even though she wasn't in a comatose state, her body, which was protecting itself, had been unconscious all along and still was. He stated that I should not expect her to be able to respond. I went to my baby's bedside, and the doctor left us.

Now, I realize doctors are much more intelligent that I can ever pretend to be, and I completely understood what he was telling me. In other words, Jonna was not going to talk to me, see me, or even know that I was there. I took him at his word and didn't expect anything. I just leaned toward the bed, laid my face upon my little girl's head, and did the only thing I knew to do—pray some more. When Jonna was a little girl, she learned to give "butterfly kisses." It had been many years since I had received one from her. In fact, it had been many years since those "butterfly kisses" had even crossed my mind. However, while my cheek was lying across her cheek and tears were streaming from mine to hers, I felt a twinge of a butterfly. "No," I thought, "the doctor said she wouldn't respond."

But I guessed that still, small voice inside my heart knew better, because I pulled away from her face just in time to see her eye lashes move. "Jonna, Momma's here. I am here. It's gonna be okay." To my surprise, her eyes opened just enough for me to see that she was trying to wake up. I didn't think. Without any thought, I leaned over her once again and whispered in her ear words that she needed to hear. "Close your baby eyes. Let Jesus hold you," were softly spoken, and after being heard, Jonna closed her eyes.

Soon a nurse came into the room to advise me that the helicopter had landed outside and they were ready to take Jonna to St. Louis. I asked the nurse where I needed to go to get on the helicopter. She said, "I don't think they will let you ride with them, but come with me." I was led through the outside doors to the helipad where the attendant was preparing for Jonna's arrival. I explained that we lived three hours from St. Louis. I begged that man to let me ride with them so I could be with my daughter. "Ma'am, we aren't allowed to take passengers," he replied. "Look, that's my baby. I couldn't ride in the ambulance, and now you tell me I can't go with her on the helicopter. I am going," was my response. I stood to the side as they loaded the helicopter with my precious cargo, but before the door was shut, I was determined that I was getting on board and started taking steps to the entrance. "We can't take you. I am so sorry, but you can't get on," echoed around me.

One of the nurses who had helped Jonna came towards me and gently pulled me away from the helicopter. "Come back in," she calmly said as she led me through the doors of the hospital. "She will be okay. She's young, healthy, and strong. Her condition is stable." Those words were the exact words I heard from the doctor. Maybe the Lord had given them to her to say for confirmation. Maybe that meant that she was going to be okay. However badly I wanted to believe what these professionals were saying to me, my spirit just wasn't buying it. As we entered the hospital, I looked at this dear woman who was desperately trying to make me feel better, and said, "She will be all right either way."

Chapter Forty-Seven

Heavenly Home

WHEN THE PARAMEDICS LOADED their precious cargo into the helicopter in preparation for the thirty-minute flight for the St. Louis hospital, Jonna's condition was stable. The doctors had informed me that she had broken both arms and her collar bone. Yet, once again, they cautiously reminded me that she was strong and in awesome physical shape. "It will take a while," they stated, "but she will recover." I wanted so desperately to believe them, but somehow my spirit was skeptical.

Jon's stepdad had driven to our house and told Jon about the accident. Jon had been outside on the mower and didn't hear all the pleading rings of the phone screaming for him to answer. Together they sped down Highway 13 to the hospital just in time to glance in the helicopter before liftoff. I had been under the impression that the life-flight journey to St. Louis had already begun, so I decided to go back into the hospital and wait for my husband. When I turned around to find the entrance back into the hospital, I saw no door.

All I could see were faces. Faces of students from the school, faces of parents, faces of teachers, and faces that I had no clue who they belonged to. A menagerie of people who had collected together on that little helicopter pad. The multitude expanded far past the hard and cold concrete pad on which sat the aircraft which housed my baby girl. Tears were flowing from almost all visible eyes and sobs were all that captured the attention of my ears as I desperately tried to get back into the solitude of the hospital. Twisting and turning amidst the crowd and hugging each one that I could made me feel so very guilty that my greatest desire was to be alone at that moment. My mind was trying to comprehend it all. My body was trying to recover from shock and exhaustion. Neither was succeeding! After what seemed to be a lifetime, I managed to find a quiet corner in the front entrance of the hospital. I sat down on a bench and found myself lost in the stillness of a portrait of my Lord Jesus hanging quietly on the wall. Thoughts begun to race rapidly through my tormented mind. The Holy Spirit brought to memory a night last November. A night that a prophecy was given to me. A night which ended with others downplaying the words given to me by the Holy Spirit . . . "You are facing a great tribulation. Keep your eyes on me and you will be all right." I absolutely understood those words to mean I was to travel down a road of sorrow. While others decided the interpretation of the prophecy meant some sort of trial or temptation, I knew the moment I heard the Lord's words that *nothing* about the journey I was to take was a trial, test, or temptation. The very same moment I looked at that portrait of Jesus' face sharing back at me. It was as if the hand-painted brown eyes were looking right into my spirit, transmitting nothing but pure comfort, peace, and love. Without having to second guess thoughts which were dashing through my mind, I suddenly recognized the true meaning of the prophecy: "You will face a great tribulation. Keep your eyes on me and you will be okay."

Was I afraid? Yes! I could go down the list of emotions every human innately carries from birth, but I didn't feel any other except fear. Then, as my eyes were fixated on the picture on the wall, I heard a whisper. The whisper of a voice telling me, "I have given you my peace." I recognized the serene voice. I understood the love that these words were given with. My fear seemed to vanish into a distant time where it wasn't visible to me any longer. As I accepted the peace that was covering me as a precious gift from my Lord, the Scripture written in John 14:27 revealed itself to my tormented and confused mind.

In the Scripture Jesus told his Apostles before the Roman guards arrested him, "Peace I leave with you, my peace I give unto you; not as the world giveth give I unto you. Let not your heart be troubled, neither let it be afraid." I had known this Scripture for many years, but only at that given moment did complete knowledge of the word "peace" wrap around me.

Chapter Forty-Eight

Solemn

A LITTLE WHILE LATER, I found Jon walking around the heliport. We talked for a brief time, got into my car, and headed toward Harrisburg to gather some clothes and head for St. Louis. The drive home was solemn as both of us were in a state of uncertainty. I don't believe either of us had any clue what to talk about. But all the while, all I could think about was the prophecy, Jonna, and the words, "Keep your eyes on me and you will be all right." That knowledge and my firm faith in my Lord Jesus were the glue that was holding me together.

When we arrived at 35 Spring Valley Road, the little household that had been nicknamed the Shackarosa, our three kitties met us at the door. It only took a short time for them to realize that things were not normal. Casper went off and hid. Cricket just sat at the door not understanding why she couldn't go out. My sweet Mozart was the one that followed me into the bedroom and craved so much attention that it was hard for me to pack my bag so I would be prepared to stay with Jonna in the hospital for however long was required. It was then, the moment I picked Mozart up to give him the momma attention he was asking for, that I broke down and sobbed into his long yellow fur.

My spirit was crying out as if my connection to my baby girl was in trouble. I broke all records packing my overnight bag. Jon was taking entirely too long with his and I consistently reminded him that we had to go. The three-hour drive to St. Louis was facing us and I felt we had to leave now. Because of the unsettled feeling I was experiencing deep in my momma gut, I decided to call the St. Louis hospital to see if the helicopter had arrived yet.

After going through all the different channels of phone conversations, I was finally connected to the emergency room. When the E. R. nurse on the other end of the phone took the information necessary for security purposes from me, she put me on hold for what seemed to be an eternity to find out what the status of my daughter was. An attendant in the E. R. picked up the phone and discussed her condition in medical jargon. Finally after my patience was rapidly wearing thin, I asked him one simple question. With a stern voice I said, "Is my daughter stable?" His answer this time was short and to the point. "No ma'am. She's not."

These words shot through me like a fiery arrow. Why, I asked myself. She was stable when she left Marion hospital on the helicopter. What was wrong? What had happened in forty-five minutes to make her worse? Many, many questions started pouring into my brain. None of which I could answer. None of which really mattered. All that mattered was that I needed to get to my Jonna.

Finally ready, Jon and I told the kitties we would be back soon, locked the doors, and drove away from the Shackarosa. We drove to Jon's parents' house because they were graciously being our taxi on the trip. I supposed they realized that neither of us were capable of focusing on the highway. Loaded into their car, we were St. Louis-bound. Worn out mentally and physically, I kept dozing off amidst the silence of the car's passengers. Jon's mom, who didn't care much about anything but getting there, evidently was driving a *little* too fast because in the midst of the silence, a siren was heard. My head turned just in time to see flashing lights behind our speeding car. Needless to say, the officer wasn't smiling. As Jon's mom was trying to explain why the rush, I interrupted and said, "My daughter has been life-flighted to St. Louis. We are wasting time getting there because you are talking." Well, there wasn't one ticket given, and the officer only said "Drive carefully." He could have given us an escort to the Illinois/Missouri border if you ask me, but nobody asked.

Jon's mom pulled out onto Interstate 64 again, and I slept. I dreamt and dreamt. Out of what was a sound sleep, Jon woke me up shaking me. "Christy, what's wrong? Your expression changed." I asked what he meant, and he explained that my stern, tired, worried look and turned to a calm and peaceful one. I informed him that I was dreaming. Immediately after that, I looked at the clock in the car to see how much further we had to travel until we reached St. Louis. The clock said 5:27 p.m. (Keep that time in the back of your head), which meant we had about another hour and a half until reaching our destination. Another hour and a half until I could see and touch my beautiful little girl.

Finally, at 7:00 p.m., we could see the hospital. Thankfully, there were plenty of parking places close to the entry doors. It was at this time that I told Jon what I was dreaming when he woke me up.

On the way to the hospital entrance, I told him that I had seen Jonna in the midst of a crowd of people. Everyone was laughing and carrying on as if it was a big party. Jonna, whose personality genuinely bubbled most of the time, was smiling the biggest smile I had ever seen. This precious young woman, who talked more in grade school than she didn't, was talking to everyone so fast, there was no possible way to try to read her lips. She was holding onto a hand, a strong hand. Draping from the hand's arm was a pure white robe. So white that the material glistened. "That was my dream until you woke me up," I explained to him. There was no reason to decipher what the dream meant to him because he understood. We both did.

Now, in more of a run than a walk, I reached the entrance to the hospital, opened the door and approached the information desk. Sitting behind the counter was an elderly lady. About the only thing I noticed was her beautiful smile. I asked where the E. R. was. The kind woman asked my name and told us where to go. It wasn't the E. R. It was a small waiting room closeby where a nurse told us the doctor would be there to speak to us in a moment. As we entered the small room, two familiar faces were waiting for us. Two faces that I was so very very glad to see. Jonna's softball coach and the dean of students at her high school had driven all that way to be with us. They will never know how much I appreciated them being there.

No sooner than we had said our hellos to each other, the doctor entered the room with a serious and stern look on his face. I will never forget the words he spoke. "Your daughter didn't make it," he replied with all concern and kindness. After that point, I honestly don't remember much of the next little while. The doctor told us we could go see her, but I didn't want to go. Jon and his parents tried to get me to go with them to wherever they were keeping her body, but I knew I didn't need to see her. I had already said goodbye when I told her to shut her baby eyes and let Jesus hold her.

I waited outside the small room while the rest of the family went with the doctor. There was a woman walking the hallway in tears. I asked her if I could help her, but she declined the offer. After a few minutes, she came back to me and told me that her son had been in an accident. "He is in surgery and I am waiting for the doctor," were the next words she spoke. My heart broke for this momma. I wondered if she would have to say goodbye to her baby, too. Then, after a moment of a silent hug, I described the reason I was there.

She cried harder. "I'm so sorry," she stated. My reply to her was, "It's okay. She's just gone home. What greater blessing for a momma to have than to know that her baby is in heaven?" After our conversation was over, she left with the doctor to see her son in recovery. I patiently waited for my family to return to the small room which I had found my way back to.

Chapter Forty-Nine

Grief and Joy

WHILE ENGROSSED IN THE solitude of that quiet, little waiting room, I heard a door shutting down the hallway. I looked up only to see Jon, Dad, and Mom solemnly trotting down the grim hall. It was as if the only travelers of those gray floors were those needing to say goodbye to a loved one and the walls along the edge of the cold stone floors probably had many stories to tell. Stories of tears, remorse, anger, and mourning. Stories of almost everything, except a story of peace. Why was I not grieving? Why was I not angry? Was it because reality still had not set in? Maybe I was living in a dream.

Chances are I was still in so much shock of seeing the disfigured truck my baby was stuck in or watching the first responders use the jaws of life to literally cut her lifeless yet alive body out. Maybe I thought I had to be brave or maybe not. I wasn't sure why I was numb to every feeling except that of peace. The Apostle Paul's account of his desire to leave this earth and go be with his Lord Jesus was simply this:

> For me to live is Christ, and to die is gain . . .
> For I am in a strait between two, having a desire . . .
> to depart, and to be with Christ; which is far better . . .
>
> Philippians 1: 21–23

Paul realized that it was not his own choice whether he lived or died, but the decision was firmly founded with our Father God. This was what I was standing on.

Jonna's words, "Momma, I don't belong here, I want to go home," came bursting through my ears. The day she said that to me, I thought it was only because of the drama that comes with a teenage girls' daily routine of life. Once again, I understood what she was trying to tell me. She absolutely knew where her home was. She missed it. She longed to go there as if she had already walked down those streets of gold. If a picture of her eyes that day could be painted, everyone would be amazed at the clearness of those big, brown eyes which housed enough excitement at the thought of leaving this place and being given the opportunity to be escorted through space to the *only* home she yearned for.

The final destination of her mission—being with her Lord Jesus. Jonna and Paul understood that they were just passing through time on this earth. Both longed for heaven and home, even though both knew that the choice was up to their Father. Paul's mission was to stay on earth to work for God's Glory. Jonna's was to leave this earth and be part of the most glorious mission of all—to be with Christ.

How could I be saddened? How could I not want this for her? I couldn't. As we headed down Highway 64 toward Harrisburg, I contemplated the events of the day. Bittersweet was the only adjective I could think of to describe them. Yes, my heart was broken and shattered into a gazillion pieces, but at the same time, I had peace. Inner peace that led to a certain joy within my soul. I mean, what more important job could a momma have than to make sure her children know Jesus and are ready to leave this earth?

Evidently, I did my job well, because I had no doubt that my little one was dwelling in the city called heaven. I mean, come on, I saw her there. I saw only a little glimpse of that city, but nonetheless, I saw it, I was given more than almost all mommas who say so long to their child. I saw her! I suddenly smiled within myself because I didn't need "faith the size of a mustard seed." I knew because I knew! My precious Jesus showed me. He loved me enough to make sure that I was aware of Jonna's presence with *him*. How much of a gift was that? A gift that will walk with me every single day the rest of my life here. Scripture says,

> Faith is the substance of things hoped for, the evidence of things not seen.
>
> Hebrews 11:1 (KJV)

Now, I had the evidence of things not seen. The contemplation during the trip to Harrisburg had given me a renewed sense of satisfaction. Though half of my heart had left me and would never return, what praise and thankfulness I had because Jonna had gotten the desire of her heart, to be forever with Jesus.

Chapter Fifty

Gone But Not Here

It was almost two in the morning before we arrived back at Dad and Mom's. My car was there, but Jon had left his truck at his mom's so his stepdad could bring him to Marion hospital. We had dropped Jon off to get his truck and I continued on until I reached the Shackarosa. The house was dark and empty. It wasn't supposed to be. Jonna should be lying in bed talking on the phone to whomever. This was one of her favorite pastimes late at night. Long after the lights were out, she would call and pester her brother or sister-in-law. There were many nights she and her best friend would have heated discussions over Scripture and what it meant exactly.

One night, I overheard part of a conversation about speaking in tongues. Have you ever tried to change the mind of a cat? Once they decide to do something, they will do it regardless. Neither Jonna nor her friends were budging over this topic. It was hilarious to me because they were both saying the same thing in different words. As I turned the lights on inside the house, I thought of this particular night when I came to Jonna's room and looked in at the complete darkness. Being a human momma, I forgot everything the Lord had told me or shown me for a time. The blackness of her small bedroom hid everything that was inside. Her memories, her smell, her material world were shrouded by nothing but *dark*.

As a result, I couldn't hold in the sobs, not just sobs, but life-threatening breaths mixed with tears that felt as if my life was totally leaving my body. I had never felt pain like this. The loneliness, the emptiness, the sorrow! My best friend was gone. Part of my life was gone. My spiritual sister was gone. I desperately tried to compose myself and put one foot in front of the other until I reached my bedroom, but I couldn't move. I couldn't breathe.

I just *couldn't* be anymore. Where was the peace I had experienced the day before? Had I only imagined it? Had I strived so hard to accept the accident that I had driven myself crazy? Where was Jonna? Where was Jesus? I found myself lost in a sea of doubt. I knew that I had heard the voice of the Holy Spirit in my heart and mind. I recognized his voice in the stillness of the moment as a small whisper that wisped by my ear. But now? Now I heard the voice of my Lord as if thunder had engulfed the entire house. I honestly thought the walls shook, but that might have been my knees. I audibly heard the voice of the One True Living God as if he were standing beside me.

The words made me tremble in respect of his might. The words I needed to hear to bring me back to reality . . . "She's not gone, she's just not here!"

My Lord had no intention of scaring me or alarming me. His only intention was to once again make sure that I knew because I knew. In all the moments that were to come, from then until now as I sit writing this for you, I still know because I know. I know heaven is real. I understand that a true child of the King will go be with Jesus. I don't doubt that Jesus' precious gift of salvation will travel with us to the beautiful city and allow us to reside there forever. I don't misinterpret Scripture because it means what it means, and I don't doubt that God's plan is perfect.

Whether it suits me or lifts me . . . his wisdom far exceeds the minute wisdom of man. 1 Corinthians 3:19 states that "the wisdom of this world is foolishness with God." Only through the power of the Lord Jesus can we find understanding. That night, I began to understand things more than I ever had before. That night brought experiences that I never want to endure again. Yet, that night the strength and love of my God, my Father, my Jesus . . . the Holy Spirit carried me through. He had granted me wisdom and peace which could only come from his love for me. My Jonna was home, protected forevermore. She was home, once again, in a place where she had traveled before. A familiar place which she was acquainted with in a lifetime passed her true home.

Chapter Fifty-One

Hold It Together

THE NEXT MORNING CAME early as Jon and I didn't get into bed until around 4:00 a.m., and the first glimpse of morning sunshine always entered our house on Spring Valley Road, filling the bedroom first. The clock said 6:10 a.m. when the bright yellow light streamed through the eastern bedroom windows. I wasn't sure if I had slept at all, but the morning ushered in a new day. Jon was sleeping peacefully, and I surely didn't want to wake him after yesterday. However, there were two people that I had to go see—my Nanny and my Mammy.

I had to make sure they were alright, as both my grandmothers were widows and getting on in years. I drove silently into town to my Nanny's house first. She met me at the door, held me, and just cried. This woman was my spiritual mother. My lifeline to Jesus as I grew up. It was she that taught me about Jesus. This wonderful woman of God was always ready to read to me from the Bible. I would often stay all night with her on Saturday night just to get dressed on Sunday morning and accompany her to church services. But this particular morning, all my Nanny could do was cry and ask why. Why Jonna? Why did it have to be her? I responded firmly, yet gently, to the woman who had more faith and strength in Jesus than another person I had ever met.

She was my spiritual strength on earth; however, in her weakness I became stronger in my faith. "Nanny, Jonna's not gone, she's just not here. You taught me to stand on Jesus' name. You have always given me hope through repeating Scriptures to me. You *know* that God is good and he didn't hurt her. He just called his child back home with him."

She smiled and recollected the day, just a few days ago, when Jonna knocked on her door holding a little box. Nanny explained how excited

Jonna was because something was getting ready to happen that was awesome. They talked a little while and Nanny opened the box Jonna had brought her. Inside the box was Jonna's high school graduation invitation and a small angel. As my grandma tried to hold back the tears, she recapped how Jonna had told her the little angel was something to remember her by. After hugging my grandma goodbye, I phoned a lady from her church to see if she could check on my Nanny throughout the day. This task had to be by someone other than me, as I realized that the next few days would hold tremendous trials which I was destined to walk through.

As my grandmothers lived at totally opposite sides of town, I was grateful for the drive to Mammy's. I was given the chance to catch my breath before reliving all the details with this grandma. It was seven in the morning now. The glare of the sunshine was abundant and the birds were chirping their harmonious morning songs. Every morning my Mammy would crumble up crackers and place them on her front porch steps for the little squirrels to eat. Not this morning. The squirrels were running around the green grass, which was still damp from the dew of the night. Mammy hadn't fed them this morning. She evidently had no desire to fulfill that task. She had heard about the accident on the news the night before, and much to my displeasure, she had seen the crumbled-up truck displayed for the world to gawk at on the television screen.

The first pangs of anger rushed through my body from head to toes. I discussed the news broadcast with her only to decide that I would call the news station and voice my displeasure that they would release detailed photographs, videos, and details of the accident before I had had the chance to even get ahold of my family to tell them. I stayed awhile with her and drank a cup of strong, black coffee. While we talked about precious memories of Jonna, she shared about a day a couple of weeks ago. Jonna showed up on Mammy's front porch holding a small package.

Does that sound familiar? While giving her great-grandmother the box, Jonna said she had seen the contents of the box in a store and wanted Mammy to have in to remember her by. My grandma said that it had been the best morning because she shared it with Jonna. Needless to say, tears filled my eyes. I thought to myself, "Oh Jonna, did you really know you were leaving this earth? How in the world could you have?" Having made the decision to leave the warmth and love her house offered, I kissed her goodbye and told her I had to go get some more rest before people started dropping by with condolences.

Chapter Fifty-Two

My Angel Girl

As I DROVE BACK to the house, all I could think about was Jonna's visits to my grandmothers. Trying to understand why she took them both a little angel and told them she'd see them again and that she loved them. Trying to reason why she would make amends with my mom after months of standing up to her for treating me so badly. All the logic in my over-loaded brain made no sense at all! *Nothing* was making sense. There was nothing rational to me about it. "Okay," I thought, or maybe prayed, "If Jonna knew she was going home to heaven, and she knew that she didn't fit in the scope of this earth, she must have come from heaven before conception. Did she know you were going to send for her, Lord? Lord Jesus, did you send her here? Did she come from heaven before here? You said that you knew Jeremiah before he was born. Did you know Jonna, too?" My mind raced, my excitement rose to full capacity. "Lord, she knew! She had to know! I watched her attitude change from joyful to unhappy. She was an eighteen-year-old scholar filled with artistic and musical abilities galore. We were less than twenty-four hours away from signing with a college. Her ministry for you was overwhelming in all she encompassed during her daily walk. And, Lord Jesus! The icing on the cake is why did she suddenly become so uncertain about her future career in child psychology? For years she has been so excited about being able to work with little children and possibly save some of them from their little abused lives. Now she's unsure? I don't get it! Why? What? What is it that I am missing?" After my emotional rant with the Lord Jesus, a calming peace came over me once again. The only voice I heard was my own reminding me that any wisdom or logic that I possessed was nothing compared to the vast intelligence of my God. But through the calm in the storm, I did find one more question twirling around and clouding my mind. Why did the Lord keep placing the words "earthbound angel" in my mind?

Was she an earthbound angel? No, I was taught that there is no such thing. No such thing! Angels aren't supposed to come to earth; yet, in Genesis 18, angels visited Abraham and even ate with him. The Apostle Paul wrote in Hebrews 13:2 that we should "be not forgetful to entertain strangers, for thereby some have entertained angels unaware." Even though my faith was strong, logically I wasn't able to rationalize that my baby girl whom I gave birth to had been an angel long before the Lord handpicked me to be her mother. Way too much! But yet, am I placing my God in that forbidden box? Am I limiting anything that he does or can do? I found myself saying, "Christy, stop it! Just stop trying to figure out anything. Don't you remember that God's plan is perfect?"

Chapter Fifty-Three

Friends and Family

As the little house on Spring Valley Road became visible to me, there were already cars parked in the driveway. Already? It was only 8:30 in the morning. My mind drifted away from any possible theory that Jonna was an angel. She was a child of Jesus. How could that even be remotely so? Couldn't be, but like Jesus' mother Mary, I pondered it in my heart.

Visitors came and went from the Shackarosa all day long. Well-wishers delivered food, paper plates, plastic forks, etc. The kitchen cabinets were overwhelmed by the platters sitting upon them and the fridge was bursting at the seams. Sometime that day, although I couldn't begin to say when, the back door opened and I recognized a six-foot-five blond-headed man walking through the door. Following closeby was a young woman holding an eight-month-old baby boy.

My heart burst when I saw my son! At last, my Danny was here. I felt a renewed life spring within me. Not only Danny, but my daughter-in-law Trinity, and my first grandson Dalten. They had flown in from Rock Springs, Wyoming, to be with us. I knew they were coming, but the confusion of the day had put my anticipation on hold. Now, since they were home, maybe, just maybe, my life could have some normalcy for at least a little while. Danny and Trinity got settled in and it wasn't long before his friends from Harrisburg started filtering in.

All were a welcomed site for this momma. Childhood friends who had at one time been part of our household. Now grown with families of their own, they came to be with Danny for a while and share past memories. It seemed that the unorganized agenda of that particular day brought with it a sense of excitement. Whose face from the past or present would come knocking our door next?

Who knew, but all brought kindness and love to us, which was greatly appreciated. Along with those who cared for us, the phone never stopped ringing. It sang out, "answer me, answer me," continually throughout the day. On the other end of the phone line were voices that I knew and many voices I was unfamiliar with even though the stranger I was talking to revealed their name. Often, more than not, they were acquaintances of Jonna whom she had met at her work. After all, she had been a cashier at Rural King for several months.

In fact, I was told that dozens of people who shopped there would actually wait in her checkout line because they wouldn't go through another. Do you remember these lyrics, "This little light of mine. I'm gonna let it shine?" The light of the Lord Jesus shone brightly through her eyes and her spirit. As a result, others noticed a difference in her.

They recognized something unusual, something unique that the world didn't offer. When they gazed into her eyes, they were staring into the Holy Spirit's reflection. I supposed it was these people who were calling, saying they had heard of the accident on local television news. I was told it was a detailed report from the broadcast station. In fact, one of the stations sent us a video showing the newscast.

Jon watched it, but he wouldn't let me, and to this day I have never let my eyes view what the news broadcaster reported on that day. Why would I want to see it? I was there, up close and personal. To this day, I still have vivid images of the accident scene and the actions of the first responders.

My greatest pet peeve is when a car traveling down a road in front of my car all of a sudden slows down and makes a left or right turn. Do I know that that vehicle is turning? Do I slow down or do I smash into the back end of the car? It most definitely depends upon the communication given by the rear turn signal lights on the car. Hopefully, the signal lights will inform me that the turn is approaching. Regretfully, that doesn't always happen. Turn signals are meant to be used. Communication between drivers should be a priority when driving.

Well, it turns out that by the time the day was over, I had another, yet greater, pet peeve. The simple, hopefully condoning words others said to me all day long were, "I'm sorry for your loss." My loss? What loss? Jonna wasn't lost. I knew exactly where she was. To recap the words of the Apostle Paul, "To die is to be with Christ."

Jonna was back home, and she was no more lost than I was.

Chapter Fifty-Four

Be Still and Know

SAME OLE, SAME OLE. Family and friends flooded our living room, TV room, and kitchen until the sun started slowly descending in the western sky. No sooner than the orange glow of sunset stopped filtering through the living room window, than our much-welcomed guests began to depart for the sanctuary of their homes one by one. Although the business of the day was cherished, the stillness of the night was a relief. Quiet—awesome quiet. Awesome until I realized that the house was too still.

Danny was with me, however! My first-born, the other half of my momma's broken heart. The half that was still intact, and even though I couldn't say not hurting, it was functional, because my son was there with me. I could see in his pale blue eyes the hurt he was feeling, though. That even disturbed me all the more. I was very much aware of one fact: No matter how strong I was spiritually at the time, I was still a wreck inside. Because of this, I couldn't help anyone else.

I tried, I really tried, but the smiles on my face weren't convincing. Jon was holding on, though not as well as I was; yet, better in some ways. All I could do was hold on to my Jesus. "Be still, and know that I am God" (Psalm 46:10) and "Weeping may endure for the night, but joy cometh in the morning" (Psalm 30:12) were only two of the many Scriptures that I recognized that still, small voice repeat to me. The words "God's plan is perfect" were the foundation of my life's force now. I believed that. I had to believe that. My Father had called Jonna home. He had given her the desire of her heart.

Chapter Fifty-Five

Solace

THE NEXT MORNING, I was woken up to a little eight-month-old, blonde-headed bundle of love jumping on my bed saying, "Ganma, gan-ma . . . up!" No longer had it taken for my ears to hear the precious sound of my grandbaby and see his smiling face which was so full of ecstatic joy, my soul found solace. No sooner than he had determined that I was awake, he scooted off the bed and waddled back toward the other part of the house. Everyone else was awake and stirring throughout the house drinking coffee, talking, or starting to prepare for a journey I just didn't want to think about. Today's agenda consisted of one thing. Visitation for my Jonna started at 1:00, and I was required to be there.

After morning coffee, donuts, and showers, all five weary travelers managed to keep our eyes open long enough to get into the cars and drive into Harrisburg for the four-hour visitation. As experience had shown me, visitations could be a long, exasperating time for a family. Strange faces, familiar faces come into the funeral home and go out of the funeral home. "I am so sorry for your loss" (again!), and "She's in a better place!" These repetitions were voiced throughout the entire visitation.

But what had replayed consistently in my mind did not happen! The visitation turned out to be a spiritual celebration, so to speak, a Holy Spirit-filled time of revival. Almost each attendee whom passed by Jon, Jonna, and me spoke of happy, joyous memories. Those kinds of memories of my sweet baby that could do nothing except bring a smile of pride, happiness, or both to Jon and me. I couldn't even begin to explain the "Holy Spirit bumps" that tingled on my skin that night. It was as if the Holy Spirit himself was standing behind me tickling my neck. Prayers were spoken. Prophecies were given. The perfect climax of the evening would have been for Jonna to open her eyes and say, "Momma, what are you doin'?" Of course, that didn't happen. It was not the will of our Father.

I couldn't think of a single soul from Crab Orchard School that didn't attend. All teachers, support staff, administration, students, parents, community, school board members, friends, and friends of friends. Also, employees, managers, and patrons of the farm store where Jonna worked. Illinois Department of Corrections employees and administration were there out of respect for the family, because Jon was an active Department of Corrections supervisor at the local youth facility.

What seemed to be all of Jonna's grade school and junior high teachers and classmates who had shared Jonna's grade school and junior high years with her blessed us by coming. Neighbors of both past and present came. Church members of every church Jon, Jonna, or I had ever attended came. Softball players, coaches, and umpires from rival teams such as Hardin County, Pope County, Goreville, and Carrier Mills were brought in on buses. Friends and classmates of Danny's attended. The college that Jonna was to sign with on a softball scholarship had made sure that the athletic director and dean of students represented the college.

On and on the list went. On and on the lines kept getting longer to even get into the door of the funeral home. Solemn faces? Yes, they were represented among the crowd. Joy and laughter? Of course they were personified by almost everyone else. Moments of tears and moments of cheer! Then amidst the crowd that had caused the entire funeral home to be like a backed up traffic jam, Jon pushed through the crowd of visitors, and through persistent searching, he found me talking to the athletic director who was to sign Jonna with the college. Jon informed me that I needed to come with him for a minute. As I excused myself from the conversation I was involved in, we pushed our way back to the front of the visitation room.

To my surprise, there stood a family from Crab Orchard that I had been acquainted with but never really knew, and beside them was the distraught driver of the tractor whose corn-planting arm caused the crash of my baby's little red truck two days before. Did I feel anger toward him? No. Did I want to run the other way and ignore this man who was in tremendous emotional trauma? No! As I told you before, the Holy Spirit and a multitude of God's angels were encamped in that place. I truly believe that, much like the day of Pentecost, the Holy Spirit was allowed to indwell each and every one of the Lod Jesus' children with us that day.

There was no room for torment, anger, hatred, or chastisement in that place on that night. What would Jesus have done? You can only imagine. What did I do? Without a moment's hesitation, I walked over to that man, held him, and let him cry in my arms. All I could feel was complete empathy for him. I mean, no matter how badly I was broken inside, I could not even begin to imagine what this soul was feeling. There's no way anyone would have known what he was feeling unless you had walked a mile in his shoes.

I didn't talk, I didn't retaliate, I forgave and I loved without even thinking. Yes, indeed, the Spirit of the Lord was in that place.

I don't know when that family left because after our encounter, I walked back to the front to stand proudly in front of my Jonna. Several of those who knew that tractor driver, farm owner, and families had watched. They observed out of curiosity and they looked on to see what I would do. Several came to me later informing me that my actions were exactly what they expected. Others reported that they did not understand how on earth I could forgive, much less hold him as he cried. Yet, others stated that there was no way they could have bestowed forgiveness like that. "How did you do that?" they asked.

"I didn't do it . . . Jesus did it through me," I simply told them.

The night continued on. The scheduled time for the visitation's conclusion came and went. Not too long after 5:00, the funeral director, who had been one of my closest friends for almost thirty years, came up to Jon and me. He said it was pouring rain outside and that the other men working that night were passing out umbrellas to those still in line. The line outside of the funeral home, even after the intended four-hour period of gathering was passed, was at least three blocks long. People who cared for Jonna, people who loved Jonna, people who were intrigued by Jonna, and people who had seen the Holy Spirit bestowed within her being displayed through her by the power of the Holy Spirit were actually standing in a drenching downpour waiting to finally get into the funeral home.

It was during that conversation as well that Jon and I were told that a count had been taken and up to that time there had been approximately 2,300 people walk through the entrance of the double-door funeral home. It was the biggest turnout ever recorded (I didn't even know they did such a count) to that date. The time was about 8:00 p.m. The doors to the home kept opening and those who had been standing in the cold, wet rain had finally reached the entrance and were allowed to enter. Worn, tired, emotions used up, at 10:15 that night, the line diminished and there were no more participants in "Jonna's celebration."

The visitation room was occupied by only a few family members who had held out until the last, the funeral home employees, Danny, Trinity, Jon, and me. A sincere feeling of endless satisfaction dwelled within my spirit. However, there was one more thing that was ahead of me that I truly wasn't prepared for until the time arrived. Since everyone but family had departed, I thought it to be the time I was alone with my Jonna.

Upon gazing down on that beautiful, still face, I said, "Sweetheart, do you remember the prophecy that you had when the Lord told you that you would touch the lives of thousands? Did you see all the people tonight? I know you did. These were just the start of things to come, things that will happen because of the mission you had here on earth. Just you wait and see. People you and I don't even know will be affected by the things you have left behind." During the course of the conversation, I was joined by the others.

The unexpected task at hand had arrived. I had to say goodbye to my earthbound angel. I hadn't considered this moment. I never anticipated that when I left her side that night, I would never gaze upon the little baby I gave birth to eighteen years ago. I would never be able to play with her hair again, which I had done since she was two years old. I felt my motherly protection rise within me and wanted desperately to grab my little girl and run away. I couldn't move . . . I couldn't do anything! But I couldn't stay. What could I do? Nothing but say goodbye.

Then I heard a still, small voice once again telling me, "When you are weak, then I am strong." (2 Corinthians 13:9) After the voice stopped, I had just enough courage to walk away. I felt my feet moving, and even though tears were gushing down my face, I turned and left. "I would see her again," I told myself. Yes, I would see her again because Jesus promised. I was given a dream at 5:27 p.m. just two days ago showing me my baby was with Jesus and multitudes of others. I was a child the King, and I would be there, too, one day

Chapter Fifty-Six

God's Secret

There are secrets of providence which God's dear children may learn. His dealings with them often seem, to the outward eye, dark and terrible. Faith looks deeper and says, "This is God's secret. You look only on the outside; I can look deeper and see the hidden meaning."

Sometimes diamonds are done up in rough packages, so that their value cannot be seen. When the tabernacle was built in the wilderness there was nothing rich in its outward covering and rough badger skin gave no hint of the valuable things which it contained.

God may send you, dear friends, some costly packages. Do not worry if they are done up in rough wrappings. You may be sure there are treasures of love, and kindness, and wisdom hidden within. If we take what he sends, *and trust him* for the goodness in it, even in the dark, we shall learn the meaning of the secrets of providence.

—A.B. Simpson

The last and final day of the five-day journey which began last Thursday, May 3, had finally gotten here. Friends and family who had not been seen for years were reunited. Feasts on top of feasts had been faithfully delivered to our home so that nobody would be without food for days. But now the time had come when the last ceremony would be conducted at the gravesite. We had decided a few days before that too much "celebration" was not necessary. As a result, the funeral was limited to only family and friends who chose to be there.

I could go on and on hedging around the description of this day's event; but it would be only repetition of the same meaning over and over. There would be nothing written on this paper that could explain or describe to you what actually had occurred on this day. Why? I honestly don't remember. It's as if all my defense mechanisms started their engines all at once and kept me from even acknowledging mentally what I was doing or where I was.

From the beginning of the drive to the cemetery, I remember sitting next to Trinity in the funeral home's family car. The next block of time vanished from me. It left . . . it surrendered to time travel to a distant place where my limited brain cells could never find it. When my mechanisms of protection stopped working, I found myself walking, or being supported so I could place one foot in front of the other, by Danny and Jon. Do I remember getting in the car to make the long, dreary journey home? Absolutely not! Do I remember leaving the funeral home to make a twenty-minute drive to our church where faithful and loving church members had prepared a meal for us? No, I don't recall that either. Well, you might be saying, "Get on with it . . . What *do* you remember? What's next?"

The next recollection I have is arriving at the church, where a few family members had gathered for dinner. I remember leaving the warmth of family, taking my grandson Dalten upstairs into the sanctuary, sitting there holding him in my arms, and talking to my Jesus. At that precise moment, all I needed was to hold my baby grandson, and feel the warmth and cuddles that a baby could give. We stayed upstairs until I felt that we should go back to dinner. After all, I had kidnapped Dalten. We had disappeared from all activity, and, unless someone had gone searching for us and seen us in the darkened sanctuary, nobody knew where we were hiding.

Finally, our time together had ended, as the funeral home vans were bringing everything that belonged to us from the funeral visitation. We had gotten home before the caravan arrived at Shackarosa. Trinity slid off into the bedroom to rest and see if Dalten would sleep beside her. The last three days had been hard on this precious gift from God. He was grumpy and worn out. I had no clue what Danny and Jon were doing because I was enjoying my solitude while waiting for the flowers from the funeral home to come.

I had paid no attention to flowers, plants, angel statues, wreaths, or any kind of memorabilia that had been delivered to the funeral during visitation. In the first place, the rooms of the funeral home were shrouded by people. If you had tried to see the items that lined the walls, it would have been impossible unless you pushed, twisted, and turned, like putting a screw in a piece of wood. So, I had no inkling as to what the vans held when they pulled into the driveway. One by one, each item sent with love was carried into the house.

The entourage was so long, that before I knew it, the house was full of plants and flowers. So full, in fact, that they started placing them on the outside deck. Eventually, the vans were emptied, only to hear, "Christy, we have more to bring. We'll be back in a little while." Wow! As much as I *love* plants, there were simply too many to place on a table or shelf. This job would have to wait for another day, and it did.

With day's end, and everyone exhausted from tooth to toenail, we one by one drifted off to the bedrooms in hopes of falling asleep and waking to find a new day. While snuggling under the blankets on the bed, which brought a sense of protection and security to me, Mozart was on the pillow above my head sleeping soundly. Casper was lying at the foot of the bed curled up in a ball. Cricket had secured a secluded spot in the computer room—now temporary bedroom for Danny, Trinity, and Dalten, all underneath Dalten's crib.

Jon was snoring beside me, which entitled me to some kind of a normal night's scenario. However, for me, sleep wasn't anything that was in my near future. As I was hoping to doze off at any moment, my mind kept reliving the accident. Images of that day rolled and rolled through my mind only to diminish any chance that sleep was getting closer to reality. Then, finally, the question that everyone was asking each other and God entered into existence in my mind.

"Why, God? Why? Why did Jonna have to go home?"

Even though it was as if the Lord Jesus had gone out of his way to make sure that I was prepared for the tribulation coming to me, truly prepared in the spiritual sense, I suppose that "why" was inevitable, and it had arrived. I had always been taught not to question God. However, as I had grown in my spiritual walk, I realized that prayer is only a conversation with him. I felt at ease talking to my Lord as I would talk to anyone.

Discussing, listening, and asking questions. Now was a time that I preferred to do more of the talking and less of the listening. I informed him that he could have healed my Jonna. He could have prevented the entire accident. He could have done this and he could have done that. As a gracious listener, he listened while I rambled on and on as if I thought he didn't already know what my next words were going to be. Gradually, my words started to grow further and further apart. I was talking myself to sleep.

But during this process, no matter what came out of my mouth, deep within my soul, I knew without any shadow of a doubt that God's plan was perfect. I believed with all my heart that no matter what "secrets" the Lord sent to me that he was always in control, and before the final deluge into sleep, I remembered a Scripture that I had learned many months ago.

"All things work together for the good to those who love the Lord and are called for his purpose" (Romans 8:28). As the pangs of sleep overtook me, I felt peace once again knowing that however devastating this tribulation was, there would be something—at least one thing—to show its beautiful face as a result. *Nothing* the Lord does is in vain. Nothing!

I would see his glory shine through this. I would see his glory shine. Truthfully, as I felt my eyelids close in surrender to the day, the *only* thing that mattered was for the glory of God to radiate through my life. No matter what I endured for him, HE alone was worthy to be praised. With that, sleep came.

Chapter Fifty-Seven

All Things Are Possible

THE NEXT SEVERAL DAYS came with ups and downs, ins and outs. Danny stayed for a few more days. Needless to say, when I hugged them goodbye as they departed for their St. Louis flight back to Wyoming, my heart broke all over again. I knew it wasn't fair to him, but for the short time my son was with me, knowing we were all together under the same roof during the darkness of the night and knowing that I would hear the word "Momma" now and again throughout the day, he made each passing hour worthwhile. Now, just as it was when Jonna's visitation was over, I couldn't find it within me to tell him goodbye. However painful it was, I realized he had a job which expected him back the following Monday.

What was I to do now? I found myself in a maze of cleaning, rearranging, redoing, throwing away, giving away, and whatever else I could conjure up to keep me busy. During the quiet times, I read the Bible, talked to my Lord, and kept my eyes on him. If you haven't been able to tell up to this point, I believe in the Holy Spirit and all of his gifts. Along those lines, I believe that Jesus can do anything that he wants to in accordance with the will of his Father.

Are you doubting me? Well, get ready for this one. Maybe you better sit down.

For with God, nothing is impossible.

Luke 1:37

One afternoon, I was deep in prayer. Some great spiritual minds that I knew called it "taking a journey." Whichever title you want to give it, I was so lost in prayer that I couldn't speak anymore. All I could do was keep my mouth shut and my ears open. While I was mesmerized by the silence around me, I heard a still, small voice. not the voice of the Lord, but a girl's voice which I recognized immediately to be my Jonna (No, I wasn't on drugs, to clarify). Jonna said, "Hi, Momma. It's gonna be okay." Needless to say, I was ecstatic. My heart was racing as fast as it could. All I wanted to do was talk about her and what she was doing, and what had happened. But, she informed me that she couldn't really talk right then. "Heaven is so busy, Momma. Just wanted to let you know it is all okay. One of these days, you and I are gonna walk these streets of gold hand-in-hand." As soon as I heard those words, I developed an entirely new set of questions to ask. My earthbound angel concluded the conversation quickly by saying, "Momma, you have no idea how wonderful Jesus is."

With that being said, I felt my senses wander back to reality and my eyes open. No tears were flowing down my face, only a smile across my face that I hadn't felt in days. Jesus is "wonderful," she said. My little earthbound angel knew him!

That is a type of peace that only Jesus can give. Well, this momma was experiencing complete and total calm in the midst of her storm. All was well in my small world. The words "It is well, it is well with my soul" echoed through my mind. The words of a hymn I had learned as a child. How very shallow and selfish of me to only be concerned with my baby. In retrospect, I should have only had the desire to ask her about Jesus. On earth my little angel lived for him, and now in heaven she was with her Savior, face to face. With this blessing I had just received, I understood a little more why going home was my daughter's desire.

Just a few days later, another "supernatural" blessing of confirmation happened that some of you may shake your head over. While I was sitting in my chair one afternoon reading the Bible, the phone started ringing. The noise had startled me so I jumped up, answered it, and heard a voice telling me that the death certificates were ready to pick up anytime. This was good news, as we were waiting for them for various insurance claims, etc. Jon and I hurried into town and retrieved them from the funeral home.

Even though the certificates were legally a necessity as they were certified, I wasn't in any hurry to actually read one. However, on the drive home I opened the envelope which they were housed in and took one out. All I did was glance over it until a part of the print caught my eye. I was fixated on what the print said.

Let me do a side bar here for a minute. Think back to the dream I had on the way to St. Louis hospital. I had told you that after seeing my baby in heaven, Jon woke me up concerned over my change of expression. Then looking at the clock to see how much further St. Louis was. Do you remember the time on the clock? 5:27 p.m., the car's digital clock informed me. Sit down and get ready skeptics, as this may come as a shock. The certified time of death as recorded on the hospital record and transferred to a certified death certificate by the State of Missouri said 5:27 p.m. How could the Holy Spirit have been any clearer when he showed me Jonna's entrance into heaven? Scripture said to "test the Spirits." What greater confirmation of a blessing or gift given to me could this be? None greater. No, not anything else could have caused the chills that were running across my body. "You have no idea how wonderful Jesus is, Momma," were the last words I heard from Jonna's mouth. Yes, my angel girl, yes! Jesus truly is wonderful. Wonderful beyond imagination!

Chapter Fifty-Eight

Unimaginable Blessing

WHAT COULD I BEGIN to think after Jonna was allowed to talk to me? I mean, how could anything top that? The most unimaginable blessing a Momma could ever receive had been given to me. Proof of heaven's existence? I most certainly didn't have to wait until I walked into heaven now to know it's a place that truly does exist. Because of my Lord calling his child home, I have been allowed to know because I know. Where was it? Have no idea. Does it matter? No. The only thing that matters is that heaven is real. Jesus said so and that makes it absolutely true.

> Let not your heart be troubled; you believe in God, believe also in me. In my Father's house are many mansions; if it were not so, I would have told you. I go to prepare a place for you.

John 14:1–2

The next few days brought a new anxiety for me, yet each day invited a new surprise. Whether it was going to the grocery only to see Jonna's favorite ice cream in the freezer, driving down the highway only to either end up following a tractor or confront one coming towards me, or watching Cricket smelling Jonna's room as if she were desperately trying to find her momma all brought added stress. Then, surprisingly, the next moment may bring me peace and serenity from the sweet aroma of honeysuckle drifting through the opened window or hearing a song on the radio which Jonna and I would harmonize to on the way to school. The expected things didn't shatter my heart nearly as much as the unwelcomed events that were not foreseen.

However, looming on the horizon was a ceremony at Crab Orchard School just a short time away. The athletic department was making preparations for the annual sports awards, which recognized the athletes of the school year 2000–2001. This event would have easily come and gone this year without my presence except for one thing: Jonna was to be recognized and honored. On top of that, I was to be part of the recognition.

You might recall in the earlier pages of this book that Jonna started playing softball at Crab Orchard School her sophomore year, choosing to have the number 7 brightly displayed on her jersey. My curiosity finally got the best of me, so I asked, "Jonna, why number 7? Danny's number was 71. Why not go with that one? He might like it." Without hesitation or any thought given, Jonna's answer was short, sweet, and to the point.

"Momma, the number 7 is the number of perfection and completion in Scripture."

"That's the 'perfect' number," I replied, smiling more inside than out as I quickly hugged her. My angel, even in softball, was going to use the number placed on her jersey to be a testimony to Jesus.

Soon after the accident, the superintendent of the school drove the entire twenty-eight-mile trip from Crab Orchard to the Shackarosa in order to give me Jonna's sports bag, which was tucked away securely in her locker at school. Stowed away in the large black bag were her cleats, her batting gloves, her catcher's mitt, and her jersey. Since clothes, toys, and knick-knacks had already been given away or dropped off at the church for distribution to the needy, I was unsure how I felt about having something else to find a safe place for.

Somehow I had managed to make room in my hope chest for everything that was meaningful to me. But, this well-used bag, covered with scars and dust from the baseball fields it sat on year after year, was almost as big as the hope chest itself. Even with the mixed emotions about whether to just get rid of the contents or keep them, it wasn't but a few seconds when a thought overtook my mind. Although I would still have to find an out-of-sight place, the memories of each and every softball game would have to stay. Aside from the selfishness I was feeling about it, I had become quite aware that her daddy would want them. After talking with my dear friend and boss a little longer, he handed me a little wooden plaque which he had been given by a rival softball team from Pope County, Illinois. I graciously reached out to take it and noticed that there was an inscription engraved on it.

In Memory of
Jonna Shackleford
The best catcher we've come across
Pope County
Softball Team
Lady Pirates
2001

After he handed me this little surprise, I simply put it into her softball bag and forgot about it for the time being.

Before leaving, he informed me that the school board would like to have permission to hang Jonna's picture on the wall along with her jersey. I stood there confused, and I suppose he could read between the lines because my dear friend went into a little more detail. He smiled the calm and loving smile for which he was known so well, and said that at the sports awards, they were going to retire Jonna's number 7 so that it would never again be used by a softball player of Crab Orchard High School. Needless to say, I gave my permission without any consideration.

As I had been the music teacher at the school for several years, I knew that the only other tribute on the walls of the school was that of a professional baseball player who had attended that school many years ago. Year after year, it was a common site to see students standing in front of his picture and talking about how great he was. This pro was a hero to almost the entire community, no less the students of the school. My excitement towards the school board's decision wasn't because of any pride that I carried (but, yes, I am extremely proud of Jonna), but because I felt that any tribute to Jonna would be followed by some kind of glory given to God.

"She would touch the lives of thousands" stayed in the forefront of my mind considering things that I had been allowed to witness the past few weeks. My visitor and I discussed this for a short time. He was just as moved by the request by the board as I was. You see, he was a very, very spiritual man of God. After coming to agreement on prospects of the hanging portrait, he was forced to make the half-hour drive back to Crab Orchard for a meeting. We said our goodbyes, and he smiled that smile one more time as he reminded me that he would see me in August for the new school year. No sooner had he walked out of the door, than I ran to tell Jon the news.

Chapter Fifty-Nine

You Can't Have It

Later that afternoon, Jonna's softball coach called and explained that I needed to be at the awards ceremony to release Jonna's jersey to him. After that, her number 7 would officially be retired. From the moment of that conversation, I realized that it was, indeed, a huge honor and a bigger deal than I had anticipated. I also knew that the school was asking me to give up another part of Jonna. On top of that, I was to do it in front of almost an entire community and school district.

Days of anxiety and dread of the upcoming night wore on me. I washed Jonna's jersey, folded it, and put it on her dresser. Several times I found myself just picking it up and holding it for a little while. Could I do this? I seriously had my doubts that I could pull it off. Why? Bottom line was that I just didn't want to! The audible sound of my tears and sobs wasn't appealing to me at all.

The anticipated day finally arrived. Throughout the entire afternoon, I could feel uncertainty growing stronger and stronger within me. Not that the Lord wouldn't hold me close and allow me to have the necessary strength, but a keen indecisiveness that I wouldn't be able to perform one of the acts of motherhood for my little girl caused my stomach to churn. But my doubt was overshadowed by something far greater than my fear. This was not for Jonna, this was for God's glory. Therefore, I must step out in faith and relinquish my angel's jersey.

Jon and I arrived at the school a little early. I spent some time talking to teachers, coworkers, parents, grandparents, board members, and students. Oh, those precious students whom I loved so much! Just the smiles and hugs that I received from them was a major blessing given that night. Since I wouldn't return to school until the start of the next school year, I cherished the small amount of time I had with them.

Having been engrossed with talking to those around me, the beginning of the program came sooner than I expected. First came the elementary school awards which were followed by the high school. Basketball and baseball awards were given first. Trophies, plaques, ribbons, and certificates were handed out to each honorary athlete one by one. Last but not least came girls' softball awards. On and on the awards were given for the highest batting average, the most home runs, etc. Since Jonna had played softball with most of these girls for the last three years, my pride rose for each player who had received an honor.

Then there was quiet. Except for a few whispers among the crowd, there was nothing! The coach just stood at the podium with his head down. Was he crying, praying, or just taking a moment to breathe? While all eyes were looking toward the front of the gym, the coach raised his head and started telling the audience that every once in a while there comes a player who gave more than she took. An athlete that not only played but took on the responsibility of motivating and leading the other players. A true player who not only understood the role of a catcher, but understood the game itself.

Needless to say, tears were rolling so hard down my face onto her jersey, which I was holding so tightly against my chest there was no space between the two. Coach went on to express his gratitude for Jonna's leadership and help with decisions that he needed to make regarding a game. All this eventually led to telling how she was to sign with a local junior college for catcher on its softball team and for a full-ride scholarship.

After information about the scholarship was heard, he explained the great honor of having a number retired. I blocked out most of the speech from there on because I knew the time was closing in when I was expected to stand, walk to the coach, and release Jonna's jersey into his hands. Within the next few minutes, I realized that I wasn't going to be required to walk across the gym floor to the podium. Coach was walking to me. Approaching me while he continued to talk about why Jonna's number was being retired, he concluded with asking me if I would give her jersey to him.

I hesitated, holding tightly onto that damp piece of white and orange cloth. "No, you can't have it," I wanted to scream. My heart sank to the floor, but I handed him Jonna's jersey with reluctance. I was so thankful that he didn't stand in front of me holding it. Instead, he walked back to the podium and concluded by telling the audience the plans the school board had for displaying this priceless item in the school for all to see. It was with those words that he concluded the sports awards presentation.

Chapter Sixty

God's Glory

"FOR ALL TO SEE," "For all to see." These words echoed over and over in my mind during the drive home.

"You will touch the lives of thousands," quickly joined the choir of voices

God forever more.

A moment of reflection—as with everything under the sun, there is an opposite. Dark/light, cold/hot, good/evil, and after the trial that I had endured the night before, the next morning's struggle turned into a blessing I will never forget. As you know, I believe with all that I am within me that my God's power isn't limited to a little brown box to be opened at Christmas time only. Well, I just shared it with you once again because of all the events that have taken place up to now, none will match this. I will soon reveal the most important event that demonstrated God's awesome power and glory.

Well, it just so happened that Jon had a close friend and coworker who was a baseball fanatic and knew the mechanisms of the game well. As his fiancée's daughter played ball on a rival team, he would often show up to watch a game. As a result of his knowledge of this sport, Jonna's skills on the field caught his attention. During the course of the softball seasons, he would sometimes come to Jonna's games and watch. Often at work, Jon and he would discuss her strategies on the field. In time, Jonna and he developed a friendship of their own.

I suppose that on the day of the accident, word traveled throughout the area as if a bird flew overhead carrying a banner that announced it. Anyway, Jon's friend learned about the news quickly. As he was just getting off of work, he headed home for the weekend, locked the doors of his house, and didn't leave his domain for the next two days. Needless to say, his heart was breaking not only for Jonna, but for Jon and me. He described his feelings as, "I was simply grieving."

That Sunday morning, after isolating himself all weekend, he went to the garage, opened the locked garage door and walked to his vehicle to head for work. He got into his Mountaineer, which was stone cold, as it hadn't been started since the previous Thursday (the day of the accident). It was a cool morning in May, and when the engine started on the SUV, steam formed on the windows that blocked the outside view of the surround garage completely. As this wasn't unusual, he didn't pay any attention to the windows. But, as he looked up at his rear view mirror in order to back out of the garage, he noticed an image that would change his life forever. There was a perfect number 7 reflecting within the condensation of the back window on the vehicle.

Immediately, without thought or hesitation, he knew exactly what the symbol meant and who it belonged to. It was Jonna's softball number. If you had looked closely at the number 7 from the outside of the vehicle, it was written clearly upside down and backward in order to be seen from the rear view mirror as a perfect reflection of the number. Just as Jonna had left this earth, as soon as the condensation started decreasing as the vehicle warmed up, the number 7 left his view. Jonna had for a brief time been allowed to leave behind a message for him—something she knew he would understand. Something unique only to her that he wouldn't doubt or question. This was something to tell him she was okay.

"You will touch the lives of thousands."

This man (yes, a kind and compassionate man), who had let his life slip away from God as so many of us are guilty, received a message that caused a complete transformation within his heart. To this day, he hasn't forgotten. To this day, his life is lived for the glory of God!

Chapter Sixty-One

Jonna's Message Lives On!

AFTER I HAD BEEN given the news of Jonna's message to her friend, time marched on, and with each passing year, a new message would invariably find its way to my ears. As a result of the character, love, and kindness Jonna Christine bestowed to each and every one she encountered, there have been those who have given their hearts to the Lord Jesus and those who simply think of her and smile. I have been told that women have met for lunch, neither realizing that the lunch companion had known my baby, and somehow their conversation led to a young woman who loved the Lord with all her might.

The picture of Jonna and her jersey did get hung on the wall of Crab Orchard High School. Its final resting place is beside the now-departed superintendent's portrait, for whom the school board dedicated a new high school gym. The two portraits hang side by side, both giving glory to God.

As far as Jonna's retired jersey, the school ordered two custom-built cabinets. Housed inside one cabinet is her senior picture, the plaque given to us by the Pope County Lady Pirates, and three trophies received as a result of playoff championships the years Jonna played on the Crab Orchard Trojan team. Encased within the closed glass walls of the other cabinet are her cleats and her retired number 7 jersey. A mighty tribute to my daughter, a greater reflection of God's glory.

Stories of those who have taken the time to stop and glance at Jonna's remembrances reflect how the Holy Spirit's presence had seemed to be transferred from her picture to their spirit, thus causing goosebumps to tingle down their back and arms. Supernatural? Yes! God-sent? Of course!

I have always said, and still say, that as long as I could see God's glory shine, my tribulation and the road it caused me to travel were just fine. An up-close and personal example of how the Lord works was directly related to me. One morning several years ago, I was spending my every-other-day workout time riding the exercise bike.

As you may or may not be aware, when a woman goes to the gym, she may or may not be in any hurry to complete a workout. I most definitely wasn't breaking any records of speed that morning. I had noticed the new face of another lady walk through the door, put down her things, and go to a treadmill. She didn't seem to be going at a competition's pace either. Slowly but surely, we just kept the laid-back momentum which both had begun our regimen with. Slowly but surely, those with added endurance and speed filtered out of the gym after completion of their gym time. As a result, the final two occupants were the new-faced lady and me.

We introduced ourselves, and after the course of general topics such as where we lived, where we worked, our family, and our pets, there was a lull in discussion. The lady evidently had been thinking about the fact that I used to be a music teacher at Crab Orchard School because she, once again, started talking. She said she had attended a high school basketball game at that school a few Friday nights ago and had a really enjoyable time.

I noticed the gentle woman's voice start cracking as she was telling me about a beautiful young woman's picture hanging on the wall beside the gym doors:

"I noticed others looking at these two glass cases on the wall, so as soon as they left, I decided to look closer. I had seen them when I first got to the game, but all I had on my mind then was to find a seat in the bleachers. When I stood in front of the glass cases, the first thing I noticed was her beautiful eyes. It was as if she was looking at me—into my soul. As a result, I felt a sense of peace come over me. You see, my family had been going through a pretty hard time. I thought going to the game might lift my spirits. It did, but not the way I imagined. The peace I felt continued with me for several days.

"As soon as I went back into the gym and sat down, I asked the man sitting next to me if he knew that woman whose picture was hanging outside. 'Yes,' he replied, 'I sure did.' Then, he proceeded to tell me about a car accident the girl had several years ago." Can you imagine the next question she asked?

"When you worked there, did you know her?" I'll bet you can also imagine the excitement that rose within me! I calmly answered, "Yes, I did. She's my daughter."

The woman's cracking voice remained while tears flowed down her cheeks. Because of this statement, our conversation was led to talking about the accident, trip to St. Louis, and funeral home visitation. "How can you smile and talk about this as you do? I don't see how you could be smiling," she firmly stated. Okay, there it was. There was my open door to talk about Jesus. There was my opportunity to speak of his love for all of us. There was another mission accomplished by my *earthbound angel*. Chalk up one more for the glory of God!

Another example was just about a year ago when I was sitting at the front desk where I have worked the last four years; a woman came into the veterinary clinic to pick up something for her fur baby. I didn't recognize her, so I assumed her to be a new client. Because of my assumption, I asked her if she had been there before. "I need to open an account for you. Do you have a few minutes to help me set one up?" I asked. She said she wasn't in any hurry, so I asked her name, address, telephone number, etc. As soon as I asked her the address for her account, my ears perked up as she answered "Crab Orchard, Illinois."

No more needed to be said. I told her that I had taught music there for nine years, and loved it there. Next words? She said that she loved going to the gym and looking at a picture of a girl who went to school there. "This girl was a catcher on the softball team a long time ago. I just feel like Jesus really loves me when I look at her."

"He does love you," I informed her. "Did you know the girl in the picture?"

"No," she stated, "Did you?" I felt a smile form within my heart which reflected on my face as I felt my expression beam with joy.

"Yes, I did. She was my daughter," I told her. The young woman stared at me with tears in her eyes as she said, "She must have been a Christian girl. I see Jesus in her." Well, now we were both wiping tears from our eyes as we continued to talk about the Lord Jesus. After the woman left, all I could do was give him my praise for another report of my angel's accomplishment for God's glory.

Chapter Sixty-Two

Earthbound Angel

As THE YEARS ROLL on, I still miss my Jonna. This woman who was once the desire of my heart left this earth and entered the gates of heaven with a blaze of glory. Someone who holds a special place within my life revealed to me many years ago that Jonna's desire of her heart was granted in a mighty way. Perhaps in a way that helps fulfill the prophecy given that she would "touch the lives of thousands," or maybe in a way that fulfilled her desire help take care of little ones through a career in child psychology. Either way, my baby and God's child was seen in heaven holding a baby in each arm and around her children of all ages were either sitting or standing. Needless to say, all the children were happy, giggling, and smiling. Needless to say, Jonna Christine Shackleford was taking care of little ones.

We, in our limited scope of knowledge, have come to the conclusion that we have everything figured out through what we reason by experience, what we can see, touch, feel, smell, or hear through emotions, what we can calculate through math and science, or what we can remember through Sunday School lessons, church, and the Bible. What we fail to remember or choose to forget is that the Lord of all creation has no limit. All of creation was brought to life through his breath and nothing more. Can science prove this or can logic justify it? Of course not, and neither can you or I.

Can I prove that my little girl was an earthbound angel? Do I dare try to reason why she was called home at the age of eighteen? Definitely not! Because I can't, I don't try. However, I *can* tell you that there were incidents within my daughter's life that were beyond the scope of reality of the mere mortal mind.

You might say this momma is as crazy as I can be and to some extent I would agree with you. But amidst all my craziness lies one constant . . . one stable key to my existence. This is my Jesus! He alone is *everything*! He loved me enough to make sure that I was prepared for the unknown. Even now, he loves me enough to use me as his instrument in sharing the witness he bestowed upon my little girl. Am I crazy? Earthbound angels? Really?

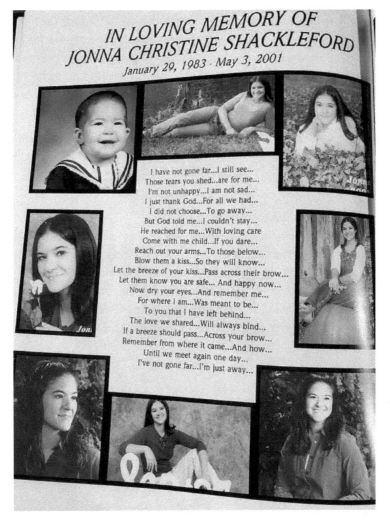

IN LOVING MEMORY OF
JONNA CHRISTINE SHACKLEFORD
January 29, 1983 - May 3, 2001

I have not gone far...I still see...
Those tears you shed...are for me...
I'm not unhappy...I am not sad...
I just thank God...For all we had...
I did not choose...To go away...
But God told me...I couldn't stay...
He reached for me...With loving care
Come with me child...If you dare...
Reach out your arms...To those below...
Blow them a kiss...So they will know...
Let the breeze of your kiss...Pass across their brow...
Let them know you are safe... And happy now...
Now dry your eyes...And remember me...
For where I am...Was meant to be...
To you that I have left behind...
The love we shared...Will always bind...
If a breeze should pass...Across your brow...
Remember from where it came...And how...
Until we meet again one day...
I've not gone far...I'm just away...

This page was placed in the Crab Orchard High School 2000–2001 yearbook by the 2001 Junior Class. Their love for Jonna will never be forgotten!
—Mrs. Shack

To everything there is a season,
A time for every purpose under heaven:
A time to be born,
And a time to die;
…A time to weep,
And a time to laugh.

Ecclesiastes 3

What I do know is that regardless of why my Jonna was sent here to earth, her life was spent for the glory of God. Her time on this planet was purposed to leave behind a testimony that would "touch the lives of thousands" and never be forgotten. But, isn't that the purpose for each and every one of us? Everything is for God's glory whether we understand or not. We were created to glorify our Father because he loves us. He loves us so much that he watched his only Son die on the cross as our perfect sacrifice.

For God so loved the world that he gave his only begotten Son, that whosoever believeth in him should not perish but have everlasting life.

John 3:16

Yes! That's my Father and that's my Jesus!

Jonna came here to spread this message, and to the best of my belief she accomplished the task with flying colors. God's glory and his light shone through her in such a brilliant way that all could see. She is still my baby and she is always his child. I believe all things are possible through the almighty power of the Almighty God. I know that Jonna Christine Shackleford will never be forgotten and her life as a mortal will always be remembered.

She is and always will be my earthbound angel.

Earth Bound Angel

Occasionally, we are graced with the presence of an earthbound angel. They are unable to stay with us for long, but while they do, they bring unprecedented joy and happiness to all they touch. While they are here, we bask in their goodness and marvel at their contribution to the world. When they leave, we are left with the devastation that comes with losing such a wonderful being. But we must remember . . . the earthbound angels are not ours to keep. They are ours to enjoy, learn from, and behold until they return home.

—Unknown

CPSIA information can be obtained
at www.ICGtesting.com
Printed in the USA
LVHW081503030921
696214LV00008B/14